Fallout from the Workforce

Living in a post-career world and the people who teach us

Marcella Van Oel

Contents

Acknowledgements

This little snapshot in time consumed a couple years in production. Along the way I've had some pretty significant moral support from friends who just happen to be some of the finest listeners anywhere. Ever mindful of my fragile state they would gently help me consider another point of view and keep reminding me to believe it's all worth it.

Thanks go to Linda Corey for suggesting the first working title, How to Manage Your Fall, and giving me that initial, unforgettable light bulb moment. Last summer's writing group participants served as a perfectly timed pit stop to get some feedback for the early versions of a few chapters. Michael Jacobs, Lee Seese, and Linda Katz graciously gave me plenty to consider as I kept piecing it together. Then there are the folks, several of whom met me for the first time, who let me interview them and use their thoughts to fill my pages. Thank you so much for your stories. It is a wholly unquantifiable phenomenon to recognize the power of shared experiences. You helped me in ways I don't completely understand. I'm sure of that.

And to my wise man on top of the mountain, Steve Van Oel, thank you for clearing a space and letting me just be. I don't know how you do it…all is love and gratitude.

Introduction

I wrote the book I most wanted to read because I could not find anything that talked about this topic in a way that made me want to listen. Years earlier I'd purchased a book that by all appearances would have given the subject of work loss a thorough overview, but I couldn't finish reading it. There was no redeeming commentary after a long-winded recitation of events traveling in and out of the lives of people from one end of the country to the other. It included people from many industries and types of work, but in the end it felt empty of real substance for caring about or understanding people. It was as if the reader was intended to be a passive observer watching a movie. The content easily allowed you to leave the theater. I wanted to understand why the failed economy was so normalized and accepted. I couldn't wait any longer so I started writing.

Something was missing from the most common public discourse about those struggling with the loss of work. As a major source of identity, work encompasses so much more than a job or career. At its best, work is chosen because it reflects a purpose for which one feels well suited. It integrates all the other pieces of a life, and yet the repercussions of its loss are so often cast simply as trouble paying bills or the need to make adjustments in daily living. Many other underpinnings of well-being are profoundly disrupted, but rarely get treated with the same interest. Issues of loss, grief, and alienation from social ties can eclipse financial worries in the space between engagements if you are the contingent workforce. I wanted to take a critical look at this phenomenon rather than just bemoan the results of endless coping.

I've included the observations of other people so that the story would gain a broader perspective. I sought to understand a growing sense of disconnect between the world as it is presented by pundits and the media, and how the unemployed experience it. How do they cope, how does this affect how they see themselves, and what do they do about it? While trying to answer these questions, I purposely left many details vague or generic so that the focus would not be on specific companies or the people who once worked for them. The discussions and observations were intended to center more on behaviors, tendencies, and consequences. I promised my interviewees confidentiality. I used pseudonyms occasionally. Their stories revealed the differences and similarities between individuals as they decide how to apply their talents to the venues available to them.

From the first day I started this project I've battled the flood of biochemistry from every thought and emotion this topic wells up in me. Like trying to be a good parent, I wanted to use discipline when necessary, calm fears, and heal wounds. It meant keeping a little distance when I was too close. I have felt obliged to tone down the emotional component in favor of something that might come across as cool and well-reasoned. But of course, the impulse to talk about job loss and recovery comes from a place that is anything but cool.

I had to maintain a perspective that enabled me to provide more than a compilation of emotional responses. As the unemployed come to terms with what feels like a personal failure, they're grappling with what they've been told about why they were let go. This may include details that were previously withheld from them. It takes huge amounts of inner resolve to quell the overwhelming sense of vulnerability. I feared I'd be seen as little more than a middle-aged woman bemoaning circumstances. On the other hand, my disbelief in the supremacy of individual agency wouldn't allow me to ignore the influence of other contributing factors. North American culture would prefer that we believe joblessness is completely our own problem independent of larger forces beyond our control. Nonetheless, I had to determine how to manage this burden. At some point I stopped looking at my job search efforts as failures. I started to look more broadly at the petri dish of society in general, and greater detail about this predicament came into focus.

From the lonesome, solitary process of looking for work, my inward-focused sense of disappointment gradually turned outward and I recognized a greater heartbreak. There wasn't anything more to be learned from my struggle. My anecdotal experiences supported what I already suspected to be true about how hard it was to find work. What could be done with this knowledge? If I couldn't overcome these circumstances, I had to understand their ramifications for how they might shape my future. I understood workplaces are not meant to be democratic, but their power over my well-being was too great. To accept that this hardship was solely my own felt as if I was colluding with an invisible force against my better judgment. If I couldn't work for someone else, I wondered if I could be self-employed. Even so, I'd still have to be known well enough to be hired. The component parts of the conundrum were always the same. I was just one of millions dealing with this, and I was convinced there was a way to talk about it that exposed a greater, more nuanced picture than what was typically presented.

Over a period of years I chronicled the cycles of my contract employment. In all those notebooks was now a history of disappointments, confusion, and striving to stay strong enough to merit another job offer. But after riding the waves for nearly ten years, the emotional erosion was taking its toll. Eventually, I came to a point of near standstill. I knew I didn't have the mojo anymore. I was no longer a constantly replenishing spring of ideas, confidence, and desire to learn. I felt used up. The words that came out of my mouth during any job interview—I couldn't even tell you what they were. It began to feel as if my personal history was little more than a story of planned obsolescence. On top of all that I made the unpardonable sin of getting older. Now, was I facing age discrimination, too?

In my state of spiritual paralysis some gnawing, droning white noise kept an unsettled energy circulating through me. I was immersed in this as the defining feature of my life, like so many other people. Even so, in order to prevail over these circumstances I was still on my own to discover the remedy. I wanted to work from a larger point of view, but how was I going to talk about this convincingly on behalf of those who felt as I did and often fared much worse? I was hardly in a position to know better, but my desire to evolve continued. Moving through the quagmire meant admitting to indignant feelings. It meant relinquishing a lot of stuff that stood between me and facing reality. It is challenging to come to terms with the shame you don't even know you carry. What was the essential misalignment I was dealing with? Embarrassingly, I dealt with childish questions like: Is it me, or is it them? Years of constant emotional processing reformed my world view and my outlook on life in a way I could not have predicted. I lost layers of identity that didn't seem to matter anymore. At last, I was a free agent in a truer sense, with no more connections to staffing agencies, recruiters, or the unemployment office.

By the time I got to the end of all my letting go I was a very different person. Yet refreshingly, I was the same person I'd always been. It was as if I had painfully stripped away the acquired social veneer needed to create the person I thought others wanted me to be. I didn't even know that's what I was doing. I wasn't aware of the acquiring or the stripping. In the end I was still the same self. I stopped fearing what I was learning about myself and began to accept the truth of life as I was living it.

Truth for me would be found in those things that never change. I would stop the unending chase to satisfy requirements made by potential employers. The enduring value I sought wouldn't come from reinventing the wheel. I wanted just to emerge from the sea of contradictions continuously presented to those at the mercy of the job search industry.

And so, *Fallout from the Workforce* recounts the years leading up to a disconnect from the world I thought I understood, and includes my attempts to learn from others, hear their stories, and begin again with a healthier state of mind. During my research, I found consolation in the intelligence of those willing to pay attention and help the rest of us connect the dots of our disjointed lives. Those I studied remind us that there are still ways to stay whole and sane, and they have nothing to do with believing the tawdry values constantly presented to us.

The first couple of chapters discuss the years I spent trying to establish a firm hold in a career that just didn't happen as successfully as I had hoped. Optimism was progressively replaced with its opposite. The search was on for ways to make a mid-course correction. In chapter three, I sampled the narratives of other folks experiencing the same quandaries as I had every step of the way. I empathized with their experiences. After hearing their stories in that level of detail, it seemed only fair to turn the spotlight to the theater of societal expectations. In chapter four, "Pundits and power" I take a multi-faceted view of the pressures to manage the ever morphing environment of the labor market. Those pressures come from career counseling advice and the social environment of typical workplaces. It speaks to the difficulty people experience in attempting to address the dysfunction maintained by capitalist dictates. In chapter five, "Rescuers and reasoners," I found dozens of people, journalists, psychologists, philosophers, healers, and seekers of all kinds, expressing the most well-reasoned arguments for understanding common absurdities. They helped me cut through the noise and put my head back together again.

Chapter one
Transitions, turnstiles and pit stops: The contingent workforce

My story is one of making observations about the vagaries of a fractured, inconsistent trail of employment after leaving years of stability. It starts out in a typical manner for many post-college kids of my generation.

I came out of the old school, liberal arts, public university system. It was fine as far as I took it, but in retrospect my experience in many ways amounted to four years of extended high school. I was still too undeveloped personally to have created any solid vocational direction. So I was just damn lucky to have moved to a west coast city to begin my adulthood. If you need to know what your options are you might as well be in an environment of choices. A large metropolis would serve that purpose better than a small college town.

I spent years passing through various clerical and administrative jobs until I decided to turn a hobby into a vocation. I went at it steadily with full-time work and part-time school. I can't honestly say that I had a plan or even an idea of how this would turn into career. I was learning what I wanted to know; nothing else mattered. I was taking my love of textiles and sewing and preparing myself to enter "the industry"—a phrase my instructors used with great reverence. I was a serious student of my craft, and even years into it, feared that I would be seen as a dilettante. This is one of the few good laughs I have at myself, as I realized much later how well prepared I was for the environment I was about to enter. By the time I began my career trajectory working in the sportswear industry, I had a degree and years of experience that included operating a custom design shop.

This choice of occupational path was deeply rooted in a longstanding knowledge base. It took advantage of my artistic skills, visual/spatial understanding, esthetic valuations, and mechanical specifications in the material world—all the features of work that seemed most in alignment with my strengths. So naturally I assumed that I could reasonably make decent future decisions based on some combination of innate skill, formal education, and desire to prove myself as evidenced in what I'd produced in the course of my education. I also completely embraced the idea that being self-taught would be just as valuable in taking the first few steps of a new career. I saw myself as creating a foundation, and if I developed it steadily over a period of time an equivalent attainment would surely follow. What I didn't know and couldn't have foreseen was how easily my progress stalled when the duration of my employment was repeatedly interrupted.

When I left the apparel industry for good, I had been feeling restless for a long time. By exchanging one company for another I thought I was reinvigorating my motivation. The grass was not greener on the other side of the fence. The stimulation of a new environment meant only that I was learning the norms of another corporate culture, not an improved way of working. I characterized my feelings as boredom, but that didn't really capture what was going on. I needed a change, and didn't know how to make it without alienating myself from the work I once loved. I didn't fully realize what my boredom was telling me about myself or the situation. Nonetheless, I was heartbroken that the field I had chosen would not ultimately be the one I'd stay with indefinitely. In the end, it was just time to go. I had a pocketful of ideas and no real knowledge about how to transition. I didn't really have a plan B, but a cluster of exploratory classes seemed like a reasonable place to start.

Initially, I was thrilled to take the leap into school again. I didn't necessarily want a new degree. I wanted to learn enough in a cluster of related skills to launch myself in a new direction regardless of which industry used my new talents. At the time I did not fully appreciate how different my future experiences would be from the previous ten years. I didn't foresee how challenging it would be to keep up with burgeoning technologies. My maladaptation to the continuous on/off cycles of contract work took its toll. The erosion of a sense of security bit by bit robbed me of confidence every time I needed to find another job.

My working life became a series of positions most of which were contracted through a variety of staffing agencies. I wasn't necessarily increasing my skills from having all these experiences. Careful reflection reveals that what I was really learning was how ineffective organizations are at treating temporary or contractual hires.

When a new person is brought in there is so much that needs to be communicated about norms and expectations. For the most part, the methodology for doing this is left unidentified and often ends up characterized in abstract terms. Thus, an intelligent, self-directed person learns the hard way what is not accepted and then the teachable moment occurs. Who is entrusted with establishing the correct version? The company has a set of expectations and the new hire has one, but who will hand down a legacy of knowledge that cannot be encapsulated in a week's worth of ad hoc instruction? Who has the time to take to figure it out other than on the fly? Things take time, but that is an element of human scale that doesn't jive with the veneration of instant gratification. And so the new hire is constantly challenged to start building a complete picture of the day to day nature of the business, including understanding its history and every relationship of the staff to the clients as well as the number of services and events it sponsors. Is there any level of investigation or curiosity that will be sufficient to give you a complete understanding? There is no such thing as complete understanding. As a new hire, you have to derive confidence out of thin air.

In some environments, I didn't realize how normalized certain behaviors had become. A quick turnaround, deadline driven workplace can simply mean that a wave of chaos is never far from cresting over your head, forcing you to put out fires instead of making well-conceived improvements that might help everyone function better.

Another thorny issue involves the territory of full-time, permanent employee in relation to temp staff. The divisions of power and authority are very dicey. You can pretty much assume that as the temp any time there is a mishap blame will be assigned and someone else gets to decide how the official story gets written. You are just the hired hand required to perform your tasks and hold tight to whatever level of integrity you can manage in the face of creeping, sometimes sudden ambiguity. By the time you realize you were left out of the loop, it is too late and there is not a colleague in sight that has anything invested in being your advocate.

The positive traits of being self-directed and taking initiative are no substitute for working in partnership with someone who really cares about you knowing the cultural norms of the work environment. If you've got a mentor you stand a better chance of landing at that mythical place called "the same page."

And yet being so public and visible you have to be the entrusted expert from the moment you arrive. This level of expectation is unwavering despite all the unspoken details that get left in someone else's memory. Everyone is expected to be a manager. Responsibility circulates but where it begins and ends is only truly in the hands of those who have the power to decide who stays and who goes. That's the crux, the turning point. We can't really talk about mismanagement unless we can be honest about the use of power.

It appears that no one has a prototype in mind. It is as if they've never had a new hire before. The attitude toward temporary, short-time employees automatically relegates them to a lesser status. This invisible handicap contaminates the whole operation. Why take the time to absorb anyone properly into the team when they'll probably be history by next quarter? On the part of the new hire, there is always danger in taking matters into your own hands. A more proactive stance may appear to be claiming authority, even if it is yours to claim, but there will always be someone ready to cry foul at your actions.

There were times when a tenuous situation forced me to take quick, decisive action in the face of a dynamic I had no skills to surmount. In the few times when I made the decision to leave it was usually as a way to say: enough. I resent being put in a situation where I am in the middle of a problem that is not really mine to solve, or shouldn't be. The decision of management has put me here and I can choose to cope or bow out, and the only way I know how to solve it is to leave. I don't have the courage to challenge you and you know it. I am becoming aware that I am so easily replaceable and this is exactly the reason why. I'm digging in my heels in the wrong dirt.

I didn't look back. I didn't fight.

There are many varieties of learned helplessness. I was mistaking my stubbornness for virtue. I kept going out and finding new gigs, never knowing if the quality or quantity of them would be better, different, or longer lasting. I was getting used to it, thinking of myself as a free agent, but feeling anything but free. Like not seeing the forest for the trees, I was too involved in the details of the problem to look at the situation as a whole. I was learning and reinforcing poor mental habits. Whatever makes you feel weak and controlled by forces you cannot change robs you of a vital force, not just ego or pride, but the vitality of connection to all those around you with whom you share and depend.

In one instance I was threatened mid-week that if I hadn't mastered some administrative task by Friday it would be reason enough to let me go. Someone who feels equally threatened in their own status can easily be that offensive. Threats of punishment or deprivation are a fool's strategy. But we are not encouraged to possess this realization. In an honest assessment one would know that in order to prevail we have to connect deeply with the work we share and hold together in common. By keeping each other at a distance we can't function well; that is the true nature of what is lost. Yet in general, people still believe that as long as someone else is doing the losing we'll continue on unharmed.

In the moment you are appraising your choices of action it is so easy to believe they are limited to resistance, struggle, or absence. This is always in contrast to compliance, being nice, following along, not defecting from camp. And it is easy to become this because you are already an outsider as the contingent hire. The so-called independent is left only to imagine that she is an equal member of the team, and never feels that she really is.

You say to yourself that you'll take the high road, do the right thing no matter what, but that is not the same as rising above the situation or even rising to the occasion. Wherever you look you have to be the value you seek. In a bleak landscape feeling alone, used up, it doesn't bode well. Now you've got lots of experience prevailing over adversity, but how has it really served you? Your intention, of course, was to prevail, and part of that is developing a deep knowledge of yourself. It is an invaluable skill that almost no one talks about, perhaps because it might come across as sounding too self-absorbed, too self-conscious or selfish.

How do you prove that you have, in fact, developed a better stronger version of yourself? How do you know when you have succeeded in doing that? Who will verify what only you alone can know? Not needing to seek verification—that is the knowing. It is a quiet, almost invisible transformation, the ultimate mystery of life, and impossible to live a good life without it!

I blamed myself for the status of these circumstances and now I realize that was the worst mistake of all. Blaming myself was the worst mistake because it didn't allow me to see these events from a more holistic point of view. The real mistake was in thinking that I was dealing with entities that actually had exactly what I had: a conscience, a soul, a desire for fairness, inclusion and acknowledgement. Occasionally though, the capitalist monster would sometimes let down its guard and brazenly show itself naked. I once worked for a company that even though I provided all the correct documentation, claimed they had no record of my social security number. Not only did they want to dictate my status as independent contractor, they had wanted to pay me under the table all along.

We are all molded by experience in deleterious ways we cannot recognize at the time. By this point, I had long since internalized the thought that any work I did was going to be a) short-lived and b) exploitive or intrinsically unfavorable to me. I didn't see myself as relinquishing power and agreeing to victimhood. My point of view was simply that I was being pragmatic, going along to get along. I see now that I failed in cultivating a mindset of standing up for myself or upholding standards. I didn't see that there were any. I was simply taking it for granted that this was the status quo. The idea of personal power was becoming more meaningless with every passing year, but I didn't recognize the mental rut I may have been digging for myself.

September 2008, the great turning

One of the indelible memories from that time was the lobby of the building where I worked, and its living room setting with a large television screen. The last thing I saw every night as I walked out was the latest CNN report of another financial domino falling. By the next summer the position that seemed so promising in potential was cancelled. It would reincarnate later as a full-time permanent position.

It would be thirteen months before I got another offer of employment. The position was not exactly in line with my envisioned career path so I gladly left when the contract was up. A month later, I miraculously found myself in what I believed to be a great place to start anew.

Managers in this company didn't necessarily need to have a particularly fixed idea of what made a person eligible to be awarded the role I was granted. There was no doubt in my mind that I was up to the task, and in whatever way I communicated that, it was accepted by the person who hired me. So I am left to wonder if the next manager hired to oversee the team, who dispatched me within a few weeks, was saying as much about what she thought of me as what she thought about the person who hired me. That in itself says so many things about the lack of reliable ways for understanding how managers make their decisions.

It is nearly impossible to give a complete portrayal of the repercussions of that event. I was done, completely hollowed out. The obliteration of trust contaminated my psyche in a way that is difficult to describe. The reversal that overtook me was not merely one of lost idealism, hope, or confidence. It was the loss of belief in my own expectations and even what I believed about tacit agreements and understandings. I felt duped as if my mental precepts were themselves erroneous, and these mistakes were in the very ways I functioned. I couldn't believe it was possible to be so mistakenly calibrated, because, of course, I was a responsible adult, and surely my hand in this was correctly identified as the culpable one. Really? This question threatened to make me go mad with frustration. It was the madness that creates criminals, the birth of "going postal" if turned outward, or in my case, the inability to get out of bed for months at a time if turned inward. The pinball in the machine had at last fallen to the bottom, and this time there was no getting back in the queue. It must have been evident that I didn't know how to play this game anymore.

In the years before this time my journal entries revealed a person cautiously optimistic. She was a person genuinely interested in paying attention to her skills and her narrative. She cared about finding a way to express her "value proposition." She cared about what she was told to care about. After this final rupture all that changed, and finding a way to emerge from this stunned paralysis would consume a very long time.

The next cycle

I knew that every time I was between jobs it was a great opportunity to learn the latest version of an app necessary to my work. I held the illusion that as long as I continued to reach for a stronger level of mastery, I could eventually claim power user status. I absorbed that mindset. I studied on my own again and again and again. I never became that power user. How do you make progress when you feel trapped in an on/off cycle that makes it difficult to prove your strengths?

In the absence of verifiable progression, I was just repeating the use of the same skill level over and over again and not really developing beyond that. The opportunities were short-lived. How can you balance maintaining your learning environment with finding a new source of income before the unemployment insurance runs out? You try to make your life sound like you planned it that way. Of course you didn't; nothing could be further from the truth. At every gap you wonder; should I go back to school this time?

I maintained skepticism when encouraged to believe that prescribed actions would unfailingly achieve the desired outcomes. In spite of my reticence, I embraced the popular myths of career advice that I imagined would help me recapture a place in the job market. This odd combination of faithlessness and conviction kept me feeling stuck. With no outside influence to direct me toward other forms of inquiry I didn't question any of the directives I thought I needed to follow. I didn't completely believe my efforts were effective, but I felt obliged to reenact the axioms of standard job search procedure. You have to put yourself out there, network, meet people to get noticed, let alone get hired. Write a great resume. Quantify those results, etc. I didn't realize how subservient I was to these ideas. It kept me in line and moving on an invisible treadmill.

In the absence of degrees, certifications, or more experience, there seemed few ways of distinguishing the quality of my intermittent jobs to employers. I filled my head with information and practiced anything I learned often enough to claim it as my knowledge. How then to convince someone else?

Crafting the approach

When in an interview, I knew I had to give an accurate presentation of experience while also communicating savvy about the needs of the future employer. I was developing a chameleon-like ability for adapting the story of my career development to the next corporate environment. Reframing the story for each interview kept me constantly rehashing the same work history. This retreading of the same territory had the effect of diluting my belief in the importance of my experience. It was as if instead of being boldly confident, I transformed into a snake oil salesman and no one was buying it. The inefficacy of my work search increased the distance between my sense of self and the wisdom and maturity I felt I should have had. I realized that as a candidate in the job market it is difficult to avoid feeling infantilized. Even wanting to prove your worth must be done in prescribed ways regardless of your individual style. As a friend so astutely observed:

> It was so clear in my last interview that I am
> never going to get a job again. I mustered
> all my enthusiasm and knowledge, and it felt
> wrong. The honest answers I gave were not the
> answers they wanted to hear. I didn't even get
> to the real truth. 'I am not likely to do what you
> tell me. I will do what I see needs to be done. I
> will see things that you did not see, and there-
> fore what I see needs to be done won't be the
> same as what you want. I will try to do both,
> but it won't work.' And that is the truth.

These words reflected my own sentiments. While attempting to be myself I simultaneously tried to present a version that
would appear valid to the business. No matter the audience, it
didn't work. I was at a point in life where fitting into a hierarchy
seemed humorously old-fashioned. I wanted peers and colleagues, but the idea of reporting to a single individual seemed
unnecessary. Flat or pyramid, I wasn't finding any organization
that allowed me entry. The hamster wheel kept spinning, but I
was on the cage floor watching.

Paying attention along the way

The situation I found myself in forced me to deal with competing versions of how I saw the rules of life. The only way to
distance myself from bouts of self-pity was to imagine that I
was honing my powers of discernment in a broader context.
Time wasn't wasted as long as I was learning *something*, right?
This was no protection from the realizations that spontaneous-
ly arose from simply watching television.

I was watching a documentary about the counselors and
clients of a nonprofit organization whose mission was to improve the lives of urban youth. These teenagers and twenty-
somethings already had criminal records; many of them probably hadn't graduated from high school. At one point in the

program a counselor asked one of his charges if he intended to get straight when he got out of jail. The young man's answer was an emphatic—no. His response was essentially this: Why should I go back and try to imagine that I'm going to be someone who can work in this world and act the way you want me to when that has never been my life? I'll never fit in. I'll just go back to the life I knew before. Why not?

I sat there feeling his outrage and incredulity at a question that from his point of view had such an obvious answer. And as I reflected on my alignment with this attitude I was also stunned to realize that here I was unarguably someone from a very different demographic and socioeconomic background feeling the same anger. I was completely alienated from a sense of purpose, even as I knew it was imperative to have one. My career, my livelihood, my self-concept—all these words with their nuances of meaning so combined as to be inseparable, now all seemed to be splitting. What did I have left to give? Without connection to a functional working life I felt too undefined in the eyes of others. The young man in the TV program may have never depended on life following certain rules. He rightly made no pretense of believing in a world from which he felt so alienated. What I knew about life merely allowed me to understand certain formalities of the workplace. As long as I held firm to my amiable, knowledgeable self, I thought I could be assured that the relationships I had with bosses and colleagues and acquaintances would serve to usher me along to where I thought I was going.

The young man in the documentary never had such illusions and now neither did I. Now I could completely relate to people with whom I thought I had absolutely nothing in common. I understood the rage, felt the vindictive impulse, and knew it was destroying my ability to reason or think from a point of view other than self-pity. I was keenly aware that no part of my intellect would surmount the grieving process. I was full of too much knowing, not enough understanding, and absolutely no accepting. There was no plea I could make to save myself from relentless self-examination. Was I too passive? Was I too introverted? Did I not seize upon something at just the right time? Did I not render service nearly enough to be seen or recognized? And what if I had known the answers to those questions? The absence of recourse was absolute, the sense of injustice, intractable. Nothing in the immediate future was going to change the conditions of living right here, right now.

Choosing state of mind, staying curious

While watching Charlie Rose interview the founders of Twitter, my ears perked up when I heard one of them say: 'Even though the truth is out there it's not necessarily being paid attention to." This comment might have gotten lost in the conversation except for the fact that I knew they were talking about the importance of storytelling. They may have been alluding to a phenomenon unrelated to how I interpreted it, and yet I felt instantaneous gratitude, and a sense of relief. If one of the founders of Twitter could admit to a sense of disappointment with the entropy of mass communication, then there was a kindred spirit out there experiencing the same disconnect. On the internet everything is a tool that will offer you a solution and promise to give you access to unlimited resources for knowledge and meaningful engagement. A job seeker swoons at the promise of the internet. It is so easy to justify hours spent seeking an inspirational blog post, a better written job description, or a new company whose mission sounds exciting. Meanwhile, without taking the time to become known to others, or even having a clue about how you're going to meet people, the promise can never be fulfilled. Would you ever have enough courage for all the hours in your life needed for that? Online time wasn't helping answer questions like: Is there someone out there who needs me? How do you direct the process of getting noticed?

Chapter two
Processing, coping

I was about to spend a very long time on a learning curve that would teach me about the attitudes people have toward work and how they feel about those who don't. While many people don't use paid employment or having a career as the basis for their interest in another person's life, others are often not so generous. Work identity trumps all others. From time to time you may be unattached, and perhaps even desire to be less attached to your previous work identity. You then have to deal with the confusion people express when they want to know you in five seconds or less. From some people's reactions you might think that it is practically rude to be unable to specify a professional job title. The social pitfalls of the unemployed cover a lot more ground than is typically reported. The purveyors of popular wisdom tend to avoid the mine field of unspoken biases and handicaps that job seekers face.

Mixed messages and the double fish bowl

I had been looking for work for nearly a year when a friend leaned forward in his chair and asked with the utmost, deadpan earnestness, "Do you *want* to work?" I mentally inhaled just enough of that question to know I'd better tread lightly. It would have been way too easy to fire hose his side of the room with indignant comebacks and sarcastic remarks. I gave in to what I already knew to be true. His question reflected that big gray thing that can't speak for itself. If you don't have the validation of a paycheck for a length of time considered just too long, then surely you couldn't possibly want it that badly. If I had tried to argue that it wasn't for my lack of wanting, then I would have had to offer some other quality I lacked, and there seemed little point in speculating what that might be.

You become resigned to the internal dialogue that attempts to help you accept the chasm between your feelings about joblessness and how it is viewed by nearly everyone else. There exists a world between the stably employed and the unemployed that neither one can readily see or fully comprehend.

I call it the double fish bowl. A glass bowl rests inside a much wider one, and both are filled with water. The fish in the inner bowl give the illusion to the fish in the larger bowl that they are swimming in the same water. But the inner bowl is where all the real mingling happens. The outer layer fish are just swimming in circles not understanding that it is going to take one hell of a leap over an invisible barrier to swim with their school again.

Acceptance, or not

At a dinner party a friend responded to my frustration about being out of work by saying "You seem to connect your self-wor…" I immediately cut her off. I insisted that I knew I had value beyond the commercial transaction of a paycheck by explaining that I would like to generate an income in order simply to function in the world. I was astounded how this could not be a self-evident desire completely outside any symbolic meaning an income might have. In fact, I wanted to distance myself from the potentially condescending tack that some people unknowingly take when glossing over this subject. When you hear pacifiers like don't worry, we like you just the way you are, it is assumed that you may hate yourself for not having your livelihood figured out.

Those not currently in the workforce encounter swings to both ends of the attitude pendulum. You may take the whole idea of having paid employment too seriously for your own good, or you're simply not taking it seriously enough, as evidenced by the fact that you haven't found a job yet. On the one hand, well-meaning folk want to save you from the earning-money-as-a-symbol-of-value trap, but they still expect you to be vigilant in the land of opportunity. You must continue to seek work while maintaining psychological health, yet for every piece of advice you receive you'll find an equally well argued reason for believing the opposite of that advice. A solace-seeking person constantly has to step over what is presented as gospel truth in order to find her own truth.

The unemployed person is heavily burdened with the need to find viable proposals for how to conduct life with skill. These skills are required for emotional survival. This is the *real* work. It is what you must do to retain your sense of identity and create the ongoing thread of your personal narrative. It is as if going to work was the glue that held you together. Without the certainty of having to get out of bed, go someplace, and throw yourself into some task, pieces of you would start to break off like an ancient glacier calving at the edge of an ocean. What you used to know to the smallest detail would now become reabsorbed into an undefinable body of water. What you didn't know is that no matter how far that glacier recedes, the land mass beneath remains an untapped ecosystem that you've been led to believe no longer exists or can't be revived. But spring always comes as day follows night and you learn how to withstand the passage of time without losing solid ground.

The double bind grows ever tighter

I spent a lot of time looking for storytellers who could calm me down. During that search I returned to a philosopher I had read years ago. It was Alan Watts who became my YouTube companion. I would listen to his recordings until I had nearly memorized them. Yes, I agreed, life is so often defined in a self-contradictory way. The double bind of having to do something that supports your life but kills your spirit necessitates that you live in a chronic state of frustration.

In order not to be caught in the tyranny of dualism, I thought it might be a good idea to keep my options open. But as I learned, framing your outlook that way only hangs you in the balance. The appeal of remaining open to new developments felt intuitively right in those moments when my personal narrative had become uninspiring. Yet holding three or more differing views of a future livelihood and waiting for a single one to surface left me feeling attached to none of them. Maintaining a dispassionate state of mind only encouraged stasis. I may have been pushing it all away. If I found myself getting just a little enthusiastic about a particular outcome, I purposely backed off. I knew I'd start feeling foolish in light of any subsequent disappointment. In my vain attempt to be detached I had unwittingly created another untenable state of mind. I would have preferred to be single-minded and intent on a particular result. I was a textbook case in all the ways that emotionally protective behavior doesn't work at protecting you from anything. I wrote a friend about where this left me:

> The only way I have learned to be free is to force myself to see more clearly the contradictions with which I'm dealing. I have unknowingly relinquished so much power and individual agency, that I've lost sight of what I am still capable of, and all the things that can't be taken away from me—the things that don't erode or vanish no matter how much time has passed.

I became circumspect about the possibilities I considered. Opinions about what to do and how to do it flew from every imaginable source. It didn't help that I steeped myself in webinars and social hours intended for networking when my so-called personal brand had no cachet. I was gifted with too much information to consider when making decisions. Shaping my narrative had to be tempered with an alchemy of instinct, desire, and know-how wrapped in a person not merely confident but who exuded savvy about the prevailing ambiguity in any situation. *How can I be of service? But of course I know how; let me tell you all about it.*

Amidst all the talk I was busy improvising a livelihood. I juggled ideas of growing an entrepreneurial presence alongside contractual, temporary employment. In between corporate gigs I would get little projects wherever I could from friends, friends of friends, listservs, and Craigslist. It never was enough monetary support to sustain me economically. Even so, I thought it had to be mentioned on my resume to ensure there were no gaps. The dreaded time gap on a resume presumably signals vagrancy from the workforce. The authoritarian hand of convention comes down hard on those who would dare be a truant from the duties of maintaining their career. To add insult to injury, I had to accept this implicit attitude that made me feel like a naughty child. I was just trying to hobble together a life between contingent jobs. And the occasional grocery money, freelance job wasn't covering my ass.

Still, I was clinging to the image of being on a career path. But how could I keep developing if I was constantly stopping to look around and see what was available? Back then, optimism was the power behind the tenacity, but I was losing belief in the value of my own efforts and my motivation plummeted.

I wanted a different story I could feel proud of instead of the truth. I had to trot out facts that I didn't enjoy reciting. No one would knowingly leave a career in trade for becoming what has been called a permatemp.

The weak cash flow seemed less significant than the loss of morale. This game was all about constructing meaning from a random set of variables, which is what it felt like now. I didn't know enough not to blame myself for what continued to look like a haphazard course of action. I proceeded in the only way I knew how. Were all my circumstances wholly of my own making? It felt like nothing could have been further from the truth, but which illusion could I live with—the one that says I am the sole creator of my reality, or the one created in concert with the world and a set of rules that appeared to be failing everyone? This need to make peace with myself wasn't really about trying to understand dueling realities. It was about wanting to find confirmation, the kind that says you're not crazy. I was growing impatient with always viewing my life as a struggle. I lost interest in framing the outcomes of my social encounters as a battle of wits or a victory over the judgment of others. It did me no good to view forces in the world as detrimental to my well-being. It seemed childish to think like that. Even so, there had to be something that would validate my sense of identity. Even if it didn't glow with optimism, at least it had to be truthful. Sometimes I got lucky. For example, when a friend's email struck a chord with me, it was as if some invisible bubble burst, and suddenly there was more air in the room. It breathed new life into me. She wrote:

> All my life I have tried to convince myself to just suck it up like everyone else. That I must have issues with authority and I can outgrow them and be a better person. But now it feels like being a better person is recognizing that just because someone owns a business, does not mean they should own me, my time, and my work product.

I understood this sentiment. It put words to feelings I had and couldn't make sense of until someone else said them on my behalf. This was fuel to keep slogging along. It seemed I had to find a way to surmount the no-win situation in which I was enmired. As long as I was stepping out into a new world view, I wanted to have others there with me. So I interviewed people as part of a reality check. Like the satisfaction that comes from popping bubble wrap, every story offered another chance to crush another illusion. Each one released the thrill of witnessing a growing collection of corroborative evidence.

Chapter three
Gathering stories, charting the territory

I could look back at the years I spent filling notebooks with observations, references to spiritually uplifting quotes and numbered to-do lists for reinvention. All could be distilled into a shot glass. With no more personal territory to chart, maybe there would be other people caught in the same life pattern who had light to shed where I had none. Here was the opportunity to take advantage of that unknown something larger than myself. Asking people to tell their stories might generate unforeseen benefits. It would relieve my isolation, and release the magic of talk therapy.

I asked a few people to talk to me about their experiences dealing with issues of career management in the face of long periods of time between work engagements. From a tiny sampling I found men and women who worked hard at creating the life they truly wanted. All of them had to face similar conditions. In contrast to my failed coping strategies, many of them seemed to approach their reinvention with greater courage and open-heartedness. We all shared the same pangs of disappointment and ambivalence mixed with a profound knowing that the future would bear no resemblance to the past. Whatever plan A might have been, a rupture that occurred in the early years of the twenty-first century invariably meant that plan B would take a long time to process, and most likely take multiple attempts to get off the ground.

The backstory beyond the commonly reported arc of un-employed life goes like this: After the separation from work the length of time spent looking for new prospects, no matter how long, often results in committing to some inadequate job option in the hope that a bridge to a better, more stable one will materialize at a later date. And when yet another envisioned future doesn't happen, it leaves lots of time to contemplate and imagine the potential of a radically different future. As one of the respondents noted:

> If I had gotten a job within six months, I never
> would have seen the world the way I see it now.

After a long separation from work a new kind of shock takes hold. There is no definitive way to control one's relationship to the job market. The considerations and purported remedies a person is left with are often not helpful at all.

> Just apply for everything. It doesn't matter what
> kind of job, etc. This is NOT helpful. Low lev-
> el jobs will not hire a 50 year-old with a degree.
> They have plenty of college kids and even high
> school kids to fill those jobs at McDonalds.

I was surprised when one of my respondents told me that a counselor she spoke with advised her to get a "bridge job" that would get her by until she could find the "real job." Even now this is a very prevalent belief. It is evident that some counselors still believe that such positions exist and will be readily available. Ask any fifty-something about his experiences and you will soon understand the actual realities. One industrial salesman I spoke with had been employed with the same firm for twenty years, and like others had adopted the mindset that finding work couldn't possibly be so difficult. Then during a conversation over dinner a guest commented:

> I don't buy this because I go past this place
> every day and they've had a sign out for six
> months saying they're looking for construction
> labor. Well, how come people can't find jobs?

And I'm going: You don't get it. You don't understand. The odds of me physically doing it are nil, but even if I could, with my resume, my background and experience, they're not going to hire me anyway. They're totally not going to hire me for doing roofing. So what does that say? What is this bullshit about? 'They're hiring at McDonalds all the time.' You know?

(McDonalds: The use of this brand is a stand-in for all companies with a large workforce easily hired for low wages.)

To be at the mercy of preconceptions cuts in other directions as well. This gentleman also had what might have been a very promising interview process with a huge multinational conglomerate on the east coast. He had four interviews with all the necessary players. Then he got down to the last interview and was asked where he received his engineering degree. He didn't have one and no one previous to the last interview mentioned it or seemed to care. HR did. Apparently, even though he was a great candidate, without an engineering degree he wasn't considered promotable in that division so they went with someone else. And so the keeper of the corporate protocol wasn't the one directing its application except when the buck stopped at her door. But this type of lapse, while hardly tolerated at an individual level, simply becomes an ordinary gaffe. The corporate face remains unblemished because it is never held to the same level of responsibility as candidates. They should know they need degrees to do jobs they've done perfectly well for twenty years without them. Never mind that eight months after leaving his company, a former colleague reported survey results to him and customers were reporting that they remembered him fondly and missed him.

High-tech waste

I also interviewed a woman whose position was eliminated

when the company she worked for was bought out by a larger firm. She was clearly a business-savvy person. She understood the interplay of time and labor division. Her calculating mind exposed situations where hidden costs went unnoticed. She gave an example of how an engineer's time was wasted if part of it was spent swapping tapes from a fleet of trucks. She suggested allowing a more junior level person to do those tasks in order to free up the time of others with a more advanced skill set. The examples she gave of her process improvement acumen were valid and elegant. From the vantage point of her position she knew that awareness of these logistical elements were not being addressed. She knew exactly where she could add value to a company. Meanwhile, even though the company that laid her off was in growth mode, the people left behind were having to do more with less. The so-called jobless recovery depended on many talented people being either overburdened and stressed out, or unused and wasted.

> I've had people pushing me to go into a particular technical area of IT where they want people to have five years of experience in a technology that is only three years old. And that's not me. And really it's not my strength. Yes, I can do coding, yes, I can maintain code, I've debugged code in languages I've never studied, but my real strength is in taking a mass of data and starting to see the patterns and how it can be organized into information. And to not be stuck by it. OK, initially I set it up this way and if I get it set up that way and I realize, but if I do it this way it could be even better....sort of a mindset of continuous improvement.

I was impressed with how enthusiastically she spoke about her abilities, and how they could be applied in terms of problem-solving. Her coping skills in the face of multiple challenges silenced my need to complain.

> Try to accomplish something. Keep in mind most things in life are not binary. It's not zero

and one. I haven't had a completely unproduc-
tive day where I've accomplished absolutely
nothing even if all I've done is one thing.

Career re-entry stalled

Again and again I was blown away by how well people coped
with all kinds of combinations of misfortune on top of job
loss. Tales of divorce, illness, and dwindling savings were com-
monplace. There were people I knew who simply took time
out of the workforce for personal reasons like helping a sick
relative, or having a baby. But if those events happened anywhere close to 2008, the timing couldn't have been worse.
Available openings had too many applicants which made it
more likely that an employer could find the person who had
done exactly that same job before. If that person could be
found, the presumption is that there would be much less if any
concern about the onboarding process. When trying to return
to the workforce, a well-qualified woman I spoke with relayed
a perfect example of how her candidacy was not considered
for that very reason:

> I applied for a job with the state. The position
> closed on the 19th and by the 20th at 9:30 a.m.
> I got the rejection email. I actually got back to
> the person and he said that they had received
> hundreds of applications for the position. He
> said, "You ARE qualified for this, but we have
> three or four people who have done *exactly* this
> job."

Reentry to the workforce in her own field was difficult
and changing professions was even harder. After getting professional certification she found a couple positions that both
ended badly. Newly minted skills weren't the holy grail of job
security even in a field of sufficient demand. She experienced
in these situations a scenario I have seen played out over and
over again. It wasn't surprising that she felt set up for failure.
Her employers simultaneously either didn't support her or ig-

nored her for long stretches of time. Having gone into each situation with eyes wide open, she made it clear that she would need some mentoring in order to perform at her best. But as so often happens, there was no investment made in even the small amount of time it would have taken to clarify the employer's expectations. Were there tasks left to the judgment of the employee to prioritize as needed? Were there quality standards in documents that needed to be reviewed? What other details were left unspoken? The employer's critique rested on seemingly vague matters like—you're not fast enough, or your to-do lists are wrong.

The simplest premise of employment is that if either party becomes dissatisfied any one of them is free to terminate the arrangement. Unfortunately, the corollary attitude to this understanding is that the employer is under no obligation to create an environment that would make working together a mutually beneficial relationship. Is this the "freedom" our "job creators" really want? There is always a price to pay. In the case of employer/employee reciprocity, the power differential is already so unequal that the employee has no choice but to trust the untested strength of the relationship. No mechanism exists that can prevent careless individuals from using it in ways that are hugely more detrimental to the employee.

It has always been this way through human history, and the situation has never been adequately addressed. Collectively our choices in this realm are as important as anything else we do. Why then would anyone exercise this kind of power with such disdain for the consequences? Presumably it cuts both ways. The dispatched employee is demoralized. The employer is at least inconvenienced, and potentially worse. So what kind of mediating force could prevent this unfortunate outcome? Labor unions will probably never regain their stature or influence, and yet at one point in history people were willing to die for them. The existence of unions was supposed to protect workers from unwarranted dismissals. What now will it take to restore a feature to working life that purports to influence corporate entities in a similar way? This question hasn't been answered. Those willing to address it are often unfairly labeled with words like socialist. Any solution that recommends additional regulation or control is vilified as anti-capitalist.

A visionary thinker in a constricted corporate world

The people I spoke with engaged in proactive steps to manage their lives and careers whether it meant more education, networking, or building a support system. Even the most highly educated and experienced person began to feel doubt about her chances of finding work when she experienced a lack of positive feedback from the kinds of companies most likely to use her talents. One woman I spoke with had a wealth of management training experience, and positioned herself as an instructional designer for hire. She wanted to include organizational development in her work, but found it difficult to launch herself in this direction with little hands on experience. It was the infamous catch-22. Like many others, she thought she could get her foot in the door via contract work, and after a couple of solid gigs continued to apply herself.

She had the courage to believe in the ideals of progressive development in business culture and the skills and experience to back that up. She wanted to work for a company interested in the whole person, but she couldn't sell the strengths of her background. Weren't liberal arts folks supposed to be known for seeing patterns and bringing ideas together? For people who are willing to prove they can adapt, would there be a place that welcomes what they have to offer? Her transferable skills included being able to write the kind of messaging that companies say they want. She also embraced leadership roles in professional associations like the ASTD (American Society of Training and Development). As a passionate, creative thinker, she wanted to be part of the solution, to be involved in strategic communications about shifting a work culture to one of continuous improvement.

> From a practical standpoint you have to create
> an environment for it to happen. Other coun-
> tries are outspending us on innovation. Hierar-
> chy isn't getting us very far. We need all hands
> on deck.

She had ideas for custom workshops, and wanted to create inclusive environments where employees were encouraged to contribute their ideas. Where were the companies that brought in people of diverse perspectives, who actually wanted a vision-ary thinker on their team? By the time I met her the blog she had started was no longer active and living in survival mode was beginning to wear thin.

> I don't have the resources not to work for a
> few months. I thought my previous experienc-
> es would set me up well for what I wanted to
> do. Maybe my field is just glutted. Maybe I'm
> not so special.

The obstacles to gainful employment morphed continu-ally in both typical and unexpected ways. For a person with a great resume, demonstrable talent didn't necessarily ensure that doors would open. We talked about how the promotion of transferable skills did not in fact transfer to positive rein-forcement from employers.

> We just want someone to do X, we don't care
> about all that other stuff. Because this market is
> so glutted they can get someone who has done
> **exactly** "X" and has a proven track record of
> having done it for a few years.

Her experience with recruiting agencies also did not re-flect the ideals touted by business management gurus. When her candidacy was submitted to Yahoo, she learned that they preferred someone who had worked for Facebook, LinkedIn, Google, or Intel. They wanted someone who had worked in similar companies who were competitors with work environ-ments just like theirs.

Temp agencies had executive assistant positions available, and short-term was better than nothing. The recruiters were surprised she was willing to consider these roles.

> Really? You want to do that? But you'll be tak-
> ing work away from someone else...because
> for some folks, that's all they can do.

The people I spoke with had great skills and demonstrable talent. They considered approaches to finding work from as many sources as were available to them, and yet the necessity of parsing the idiosyncrasies of the business climate created obstacles in itself. Whether your value in the labor market generated from ivy league education and professional leadership chops, or the craftsmanship developed over years in the trades, the pigeon holes headhunters wanted to shove you through were shrinking for seemingly artificial reasons.

Tradesman legacy and no new apprentices

One of the most interesting interviews I conducted was with a man who made a career in building sets for stage and screen. Having come from a background where I chose a love for craft in the material world, I could relate to many of his observations. We both bemoaned the ongoing changes that kept working people increasingly alienated from the work they once loved to perform. We talked for hours about how he viewed the challenges of life in the trades. (In this case, I will call my respondent Ben.) As a member of the International Alliance of Theatrical and Stage Employees (IATSE), Ben worked for theaters throughout the mid-Atlantic states for many years before moving to the west coast. It was the era when the artistry of stagecraft was often supported by NEA grants. At the height of his career with a local theater company, Ben's contract was not renewed, and thus began the process of reformulating the use of his considerable talents. After considering marine engineering, he realized the time and cost it would require to complete his education wouldn't have led to a life he wanted. It would have offered possibilities leaving him even more overworked and far from his family. A friend suggested that Ben's background could be used well in a construction management program, and he took the opportunity to increase his marketability. Then the economy tanked.

During the years of looking for new roles related to his expertise, Ben learned firsthand the unsettling expectations of the new/old wheels of commerce. Working for a retail company required a day of training in the sales tracking software. With an army of busy colleagues who would have time to assist in the ongoing learning after just one day? The unfairly burdened employee was then expected to continue learning under the pressure of being in front of the customer. The corporate approach is to release the associate to the sales floor where the customer must wait during the machinations of making returns or performing other sales operations. Management wants excellent customer service that comes with knowledgeable staff, but is inept at using the full spectrum of the talents it's hired. Ben was a subject matter expert, and the younger staff could fly across the keyboard pulling information from anywhere. The underlying disconnect was that the younger guys didn't know the actual materials they were selling or for what they were used. From the business perspective, if corrections at the point of sale took too long, the staff person risked being let go when customer complaints became too frequent. And this is what happened to Ben after one particular transaction took just too long for someone's patience.

Then there were the greater repercussions from technological encroachment in the field of set building itself. Hollywood had become less centralized as a locale for filmmaking. Soon their scenery needs weren't more elaborate than stairways and platforms. As Ben noted everything was going to be green screened and filled in with CGI effects. The future held fewer opportunities for making a good living in stagecraft. One of Ben's friends, a former teacher, also deplored the side effects of these changes when they reached the field of education from middle school and beyond. Shop classes once taught in high school were discontinued in favor of coding and other software skills.

During the formation of his plan B, Ben became very aware that a lifetime in the stagecraft trades, while intrinsically valuable, held a smaller place in a restructured collective world view:

> I made a living in a notoriously difficult business for over 30 years. I never worked in one particular place for a particularly long time, but nowadays when you look for a job it's so hard to explain that to people. I worked a few months here, a few months there. So people think you can't hold a job. Nobody knows what a stage hand does. Over the arc of time there is a career, but if you're trying to parse it out… it's really tough.
>
> Nobody knows our skill set, and nobody wants to take a chance anymore. You used to be able to walk in off the street and get a job. Everybody is specialized now. You used to be able to work your way up from the bottom. Then education gets in the way of it. You have to have a degree. If you don't have the bona fides they won't even look at you. If you can't figure out what they want on a resume…you have to figure out that game and get past the electronic screeners.

Ben and I talked about so many interrelated attitudes and perceptions having to do with work. He brought up one point in particular that represented an ongoing struggle with maintaining equanimity in the land of status and rank. He confirmed how deleterious the rift between divisions of labor remain today. The perceptions of blue collar work in relation to those associated with high tech careers seemed as starkly contrasted as ever, perhaps more so. It would seem that the tenets of pure capitalism are so internalized that their reflection outward is constant. The appearance of having money creates in people judgments equivocating imagined wealth with the level of trust, respect, and dignity a person merits. All the virtues that thrive in egalitarian mores are summarily eradicated by a money-centric mentality. It is a stressor that people live with like a chronic disease. It perpetuates narrowly defined values.

For Ben, the outward expression of these values became obvious. Five years allowed plenty of time to discern how this affected many quality of life issues. Working on weekends had prevented him from going to church, for example. Even volunteering one's time was barely perceptible on any social radar as a money equivalent. What did register very strongly though, was the sense that attitudes toward tradesmen and working people had degenerated significantly as reflected in how people treat each other.

> When did it become OK to treat people like that? Why do people think that just because you're not this then you must be that. Who's to say that person who is doing the menial-seeming job isn't a concert pianist who can't find a job? Who's to say that guy driving a cab doesn't have a Ph.D. in astrophysics from some European university and he can't find a job here?

As the minutes ticked on I could tell his view of the difficulty in sorting out so many decisions and choices had been as life-altering as mine. We joked about the glorious revenge fantasy typical of Hollywood dystopia where the rich mogul can't buy his way out of the life threatening dangers of an earthly disaster. Our conversation peppered words like redefine and philosophy in every other sentence.

> I knew someone absolutely terrified of losing her job because she thought she was never going to pay off her mortgage. I looked at her

and said, "Beth, you're an ace at what you do. You've got work in the local, you've got seniority, you've got plenty of work. What are you worried about?"

I found the most liberating thing is losing a job because it forces you to redefine yourself. It forces you to look at what's important. At first I was pissed, but after I got over being mad, and after I stopped worrying about how I was going to pay the bills, I started to relax, and then I was relieved, and then I was giddy. Because I realized I don't have to put up with this shit. And for the remainder of my contract the production manager wouldn't speak to me.

Then he said something that made me take notice:

> Ben: You try to redefine yourself in ways that make sense to you, but I think a lot of people try to redefine themselves in ways that make sense to the culture.

> Me: Right. That's a very good point, because I think that's been my mistake. Who's to say I'm not still making it? I'm convinced I'm doing the right thing, but where money is involved, in terms of making it, I have no idea. I have no idea.

Then I asked him the same question I ask everyone. It seemed important to know how people sought help in difficult times. I'm happy to report that close friends and concerned individuals figured prominently in everyone's life, and that level of caring simply can't be purchased.

> Ben: Going to a career counselor would cost me money I haven't got.

> Me: Oh, I've wasted so much money. One guy in particular really pissed me off.

Ben: That's the thing. You're going to hire these people and they're going to tell you what they think.

Me: Yeah—which is connected to NOTHING!

Ben: Exactly. 'Uh, let's see … You're obviously qualified to do THIS!'

Me: Uh-huh. Clearly, I was desperate. I was. I admit to being desperate when I did that, and it was a hard lesson. I'd like to go back to him and say: Could I have that money back now? Because I could sure use it.

Ben: What I've learned is when things get desperate, don't panic because when you panic is when you spend money you shouldn't spend trying to figure things out.

As part of his plan B, Ben joined a clearinghouse representing all the local and regional theatres as a way to maintain access to the pipeline of shows and auditions percolating through the arts scene. It was a smart move that got him some gigs. Even so, in the time between engagements he was left with plenty of time to raise many existential questions.

There's the bigger philosophical discussion that exists within our society. Why do we have to work so hard? Why can't we just be happy paying the bills? I don't think people look at the deeper philosophical implications of how we live? Why are we so obsessed in this country? Why is it the things that are important in life become optional?

And in conclusion...

Ben: Ignorance runs rampant in this country, and that's why they fight so hard to maintain what they've got, to maintain these philoso-phies. How do you reeducate people like that? To make it a positive thing?

Me: It's an entire cultural view of the world and the only people who, like you mentioned earlier, you don't change the way you think until you're forced to, but the thing is, not only do individuals have to do that but pretty much the entire society that we live in because we're sort of constricted in a way because even if we want to live differently, think differently, philosophize differently, we're still bound to having to live in the culture that thinks a cer-tain way that we're actually trying to move away from, but there is a limit to how far we can move away from it because we still have to live inside it.

Ben: Right.

Me: You know? And so that all ties in with views of money and views of how hard we should work and where we should work and how long we should work, when and where and with whom, and you can't just change that as if there are no consequences.

Ben: Exactly. You can't walk away from them entirely. I'm trying to develop a life where I can pick and choose. Where I can say no, I'm not working Sundays....blocking time off.

Redefining yourself should be about more than work and money.

Turning points without a turn

Whether or not a mid-career adult sought outside counsel, the process of considering what to do next nearly always included a return to formal education. The factors weighing in these decisions were tempting in their potential for reward, but the investment was often too risky. One of my respondents spoke eloquently about the uncertainty that couldn't be ignored:

> I like the "second act" idea, but retraining seems just as complicated. I could spend 2-4 years getting a masters in something else— teaching kids, mediation, employee relations, but would there be a job at the end of that? And would that career or job eventually just end me up right back where I am now? All that, IF I actually had money and financial flexibility to go back to school. Having given up the idea that I am ever going to fit into the corporate machine, I am now looking at who I am out- side the system.
>
> If I am not a lawyer, director or consultant, who am I? Is it enough to be a caring, loving person just living life? It does not pay any bills, but should I be embarrassed by that? Is what you do only important if it pays bills? Am I of no value to anyone, if there is no money sign attached to my contribution?

And in the final analysis she found, as I did, that the only answers that would ever make sense to such profoundly exis- tential questions come from within:

> The pros to this situation: I do finally feel free to define myself outside the system. I no lon- ger see myself as a failed lawyer, a mediocre marketer or an unemployed consultant. Until recently, I kept trying to figure out where I could fit into that old system, but no matter the title, it was all the same game. Like in Mo- nopoly, it doesn't matter if you get the doggie, the top hat or the car, it is all the same game.

Nonetheless, the problem of earning money eclipses attempts at finding a way to overcome the precepts on which the world is still based:

> The cons: There is not a new world with new options waiting for me. Those of us in the gap are taxed with creating this new system but we don't know what it will look like or what our roles need to be. And, as all the money is in the old system, how do we survive in the old world while trying to build a new world?

Throughout all my discussions with these courageous, intelligent people, I was never able to answer that question to my satisfaction. Pulling back to get a greater view revealed the enormity of the situation with which we all had to wrestle. The kinds of obstacles people faced were so rarely analyzed in human terms. Everyone I spoke with talked about the gap between those working and those looking for work. On the one hand, so many people in the workforce must wrangle a workload that consistently stresses them. Conversely, those with time and limited ways for connecting their transferable skills to available work so often have to settle for project-based contracts, if they can even find them. Then at the conclusion of those projects the cycle repeats itself. The issue of upgrading skills for marketability is always thrown into the mix, and the enticement to do so adds another layer of uncertainty to odds already stacked high.

The future can hardly be charted with any confidence when every personal choice has so many unintended repercussions. People working toward a goal in their lives aren't inclined to rock the boat when they're just trying to be relevant in the context of their professions. They don't always have what it takes to parse through all the changes coming at them at an unrelenting pace. Life in this era has multiplied the number of forces that drive all these disruptions. Even though the impact of technological changes is well documented, it is still down-played.

Technology: the beast

One of my respondents managed to keep her time out of the workforce to a minimum by adding a degree in programming to her MBA. Before getting her MBA she sold photography equipment and found that photographers as entrepreneurs often weren't very savvy about cash flow. When she was in school she got interested in tech and started teaching what she knew. It was the mid-nineties and the idea of teaching what tech could do to manage business processes was a great fit for her. She tells me: "I thought I would save the world."

Over the course of eighteen years, she developed her level of expertise so that she could work as an independent consultant.

> I chose this because I could be anything I want-
> ed to be without working within the confines
> of a title.

She's had a career long enough to have witnessed technology's march through time, and it makes her a credible commentator on the detritus left in its wake. At this point, she has a better sense of her own value in the job market, but is also very aware that all this learning has come at a price.

> I've learned a lot about discipline. In terms of
> answering email, now I've learned to let it sit a
> couple hours, let it percolate before I spout off
> about it.

During our conversation we both agreed that technology is a great tool for beating yourself up. It is easy to think you should know everything. You fall short of what seemed like a reasonable expectation, not realizing it probably wasn't. People in other roles expect her to know everything, which in turn has made it necessary to establish discipline around expectations and time management.

> As an information digester and business advisor it is an overwhelming responsibility. There is so much coming at me.

When I ask for an example of these experiences, she tells me a story with mind-boggling numbers.

> It is hard to filter through everything. I get overwhelmed with e-mail. I migrate people. I take their POP accounts, their inboxes, and put them on the cloud. I've seen some with as many as 15 gigabytes of email in their Outlook inboxes with over 100,000 messages. **That tells me I'm not the only one**. And those messages are fifty-fifty, read/unread.

This particular respondent is one of the few people I know who is not at all timid to admit the downside of worshipping the golden idol called technology.

> Technology is like sugar. Am I feeding my own addiction?

It is so easy to believe that learning and mastering are rewards in themselves. The addiction kicks in when you buy into the I-must-know-everything mentality. That in turn requires wrangling personal discipline while you are feeding the hungry beast. There were times when she didn't go on vacation without her laptop. Now she is even trying to get off caffeine. Figuring out how to enforce a level of sanity has meant creating all kinds of differentiation. As an example she uses different phones for work and personal life. The new phone has all work related matters on it, and she leaves it at work over the weekend in order to release herself from those ties.

She has seen the ego of the tech world and the slavish ways in which people endorse or support its influence while leaving unquestioned the evolution of its development. And although she maintains a motivation to keep her skills just ahead of the curve in her business advisory role, she is also attuned to the potential for exclusion of those struggling to stay current. This woman understands the patience needed to help people work at their best level and wonders: "At what point do we lose people?"

> In my field, as technology gets easier to use, not as technical, the positive is for the end-user. At the same time, this dumbing-down for the user enables them to be more dependent in the long run, so I see more hardware being wasted and replaced. (The industry creates a lot of waste with the hardware always having to be upgraded to accommodate greater memory and faster speeds.)

I felt privileged to have this conversation with such a savvy person. It is so rare that I have the opportunity to hear from a genuinely knowledgeable person about the ramifications of what so many take for granted. My exploration of the themes that would emerge from conversations with a random set of people grappling with finding work has opened my eyes to a deeper level of questions. Are our choices really choices, or are we just negotiating increasing layers of imposition without questioning why and who is doing the imposing? And do we really have the freedom to say no? But these are not the questions that will be answered by any of the pundits in the next chapter, who encourage everyone to become their own employer. If you're lucky a foray into entrepreneurship will be a fruitful endeavor. When I showed one of my respondents the website of a newly created, local concierge business. She made this wonderfully humorous observation:

> It reminded me of being the butler on Downton Abbey. Madame, while you are busy in the world of making money, how can I be of service to you here in the world of all I have to sell is my time?

I couldn't help but laugh, because at that point I felt that it was essentially what I had left—my time. Meanwhile the search for respite continues. And what are we told to do about this plight? In the land of opportunity and individual self-determinism the chorus of doing one's best gets even louder just as doing one's best appears to be least effective. And there is so much on which to pontificate because the elephant in the room just keeps getting bigger and bigger.

Chapter four
Pundits and power

The good teacher imparts a satisfying explanation, the great teacher unsettles, bequeaths disquiet, invites argument. Richard Sennett - *Respect in a world of inequality*

I have had many great teachers. I was a dutiful student of books, magazine articles, webinars, video tutorials and podcasts. The shelf life has expired on whatever benefit I was to have gained by the proliferation of counsel on the topic of job hunting. What remains is the aftertaste of having swallowed too much trendy attitude and not enough reality, the reality that can only be viewed from an orbiting satellite, perhaps.

The typical job search advisor has an arsenal of conventional recommendations that are repackaged and reconfigured ad infinitum. If you act on these recommendations you may become an expert in matters of resume and cover letter writing, not to mention all the exquisitely precise ways one can approach the job interview. If you so desire, you can be tutored in body language and the psychology of the interview process that involves a thing called energy matching. And if you really want to track the quality of your efforts then you will also be encouraged to quantify them as well.

I once logged into a webinar where the speaker wanted his listeners to identify with all the measurements of their lives.

You are the sum of all your numbers, he insisted. An activity had validity only if its results were quantified against a standard output. In life as in business this advice giver clung faithfully to the idea that the measure of a man was literally nothing but measurements. The webinar's speaker encouraged his listeners to consider their entire lives as the sum of their numbers—the number of possessions they owned, their blood pressure and cholesterol levels, their debt ratios, their bank accounts, their credit scores, and even the size of possessions as measured in square footage, numbers of cars, boats, and houses. It went on and on, and I clicked away as far as I could go. It would seem that accounting had morphed from necessity to virtue and it should follow that taking this approach to one's personal life would also prove greater credibility, and above all marketability.

As if webinars aren't enough, there are countless books that will guide you through a decision tree and help you sift through all the options that technology offers for communicating your message and vision. Everyone is a producer. You just have to figure out how to share your purpose, and above all, make sure your offline persona matches your passions. Of course, you could settle for being an "influencer." You could forge informal alliances with like-minded bloggers, write about what you know and increase your visibility. Keep in mind however, that this network of contacts you are creating is, in fact, the value of your net worth, according to one author. In the digital realm your stream of content must reflect positively in the vanity metrics. Imagine that as a consequence of these metrics Justin Bieber is potentially rated higher than Barak Obama in real-world influence. If churn is your goal, you've arrived, but you're likely to be disappointed if validity matters. How much more advice could I take? When I came upon the sentence that entreated me to "make yourself available for press interviews," I knew I had to close all those books, permanently.

I'm sure the advice givers were well-intentioned and thought they were adding real value to this thing called thought leadership. But if you're thinking from only one half of the equation you are not solving the problem. You're not even facing it. Nowhere did these folks critique the corporate state and its tenets as the source of joblessness. It is as if they thought only the mind and behavior of the worker still left room for improvement. Perhaps with just a few more specifications they could get the model right. They weren't taking into account that if you're asking a new and improved employee to go back into the labor market, maybe that person should also expect a new and improved company. In the absence of change to how businesses operate, the advice givers typically fall back on only a handful of suggestions: be an entrepreneur, get more education, and think creatively about how to present yourself in order to create and capture an opportunity.

I had filled my head with so much advice I was drowning in it. Nowhere did I find a satisfactory, fool-proof method for improving my chances. And why?—no doubt because my internal belief system was already gone. I could no more believe in a social contract than the man in the moon. Unfortunately, this meant I couldn't really believe in myself, either. All matters of functioning are in relation to one another and if one half is destroyed the energy from the other half collapses as well. You can't succeed if you're working from anything less than your whole self, and that means having confidence both in yourself as well as the others you encounter. That means you need to easily maintain an equanimity in relation to everyday social situations.

No matter my desire to rescue my standing in the talent pool, I lurched forward based on speculative actions and ideas. I chose carefully what to do next. I did the good Buddhist thing and didn't attach myself to the outcome. My life was good in every other way outside of the realm of work. My main if not only choice was to let myself be at peace with the way things were. Not only was that easier said than done, but if I had truly succeeded at it I wouldn't have written this book.

Getting noticed isn't the equivalent of showing that you can add value. Following your purpose and passions will no doubt help connect you with others who share your interests. This does not correlate directly to finding a paid gig unless you are strategically targeting someone in a position to hire you. It is as if the job hunter is supposed to believe this will magically happen, even though she is likely to be swimming in a talent pool of equally needy people. The seekers are enamored with the power of the digital world to bring in favorable responses from head hunters. Much of the jockeying for position in the candidate line up is little more than increased churn rate. It may mean that you have succeeded only in creating more noise screaming through the internet.

Such are the pitfalls of the solo journey of job search. The most common punditry combines a bizarre blend of values, and belief in the power of self-marketing. If you followed the ideas of positive psychology, for example, maybe you could feel hopeful. Even as late as May 2014, I'd seen posts by insistent "solutions providers" claiming that all we need are basic motivational and life skills. It has also become popular to claim that labor unions, for example, keep workers in a child-like status in relation to the employer as the adult authority. A proper child however, learns to entertain herself. In other words, she should know enough to become entrepreneurial. Free enterprise is the religion of those who would keep the focus on the power of individuals to shape their lives. It is a perennially attractive point of view, but it completely ignores the reality of entire industries having been outsourced. This vein of reasoning says that individual initiative alone will, in the end, win you a position. The keepers of the status quo are having to pull a lot of rabbits out of their hats to maintain any credibility with people needing to find work at livable wages. The stronger they make the argument for starting one's own business, the more insufferably glib they become.

I fantasized about businesses I could start. Of course, I did. Could I create healthy sweet and savory snacks easily packaged and produced? Design a collection of clothes? That seemed out of reach and way more than I wanted to take on. It would mean working out the logistics and a better understanding of needed financial backing. Further speculation didn't yield better results. Was there an adjunct field in the health care industry? Massage therapy or some other alternative practitioner? What about acupuncture? A housecleaning business? Sure, any one of them could have been a possibility for the right person, but planning a business requires more than idle conjecture.

So what were the latest entreaties of the enterprisers? One popular line of reasoning taken straight out of the American storybook went like this: Think like an immigrant. Be a paranoid optimist. Stay hungry. Realize that you'd better figure out what's going on here, where the best opportunities are, and pursue them with greater vigor than anybody else.

Terrific. Belief in the human spirit to surmount obstacles won't change economic realities that make some forms of commerce very difficult for small scale entrepreneurs. As an example, Etsy.com was once an enterprising person's dream where the cachet was on items produced by the sellers themselves. Now, unfortunately, this stipulation has been reversed and overseas, mass-produced items sell alongside those from a home grown cottage industry. One online commenter concluded this:

> I've looked at Etsy to sell some handmade things and there's no way I can compete on price with the cheap mass-produced glut there.

Eh–duuu–caaay–shuuun, Education!

Another common tack is to lay the source of all corrective measures at the feet of educational institutions. An initial period of learning is essential, but it won't compensate for the fact that what you know matters far less than what you can do with what you know. To be at that level of maturity you already have to possess the experience that comes from many years of work. Where the dots are not connected is at the point when all these people who are continuously learning new skills also want to have a place readily available to apply them. Any individual, no matter how motivated to innovate and collaborate, will hardly matter in a world where they haven't yet been able to make that first leap, and that requires the magical three to five years of experience. The market value of knowledge itself has slid to a negligible level thanks to its availability at a keystroke. Any internet-empowered person can source more than enough information. If knowledge is power, then the power that comes from its mastery is derived from the ability to incorporate its uses in ways previously untried. This requires critical thinking, persistence and risk-taking, but when was the last time you saw a syllabus for risk-taking 101? No one I interviewed lacked abilities to revise a previous way of thinking, propose alternatives, or listen to another person's point of view. What they needed most of all was the opportunity to connect themselves with an environment to practice their mastery.

To maintain their credibility in the eyes of hungry students of any age, educational institutions must promote their dot-connection capacity for the roadmap of life. As the advertisement I saw on YouTube reads: "When you're looking for a job in the real world, you need a degree employers respect." Historically, alignment between education and employment was a straighter path, but increasingly that is a faint memory. It is as if the institutions are saying: Tell us what kind of worker you want and we'll crank 'em out. We'll tell 'em that the degrees we're conferring on them will be respected by you, the employer. Thanks for your continued support.

Marketability using mainly education credentials today is an idea based on models originated a century ago. Isn't this akin to what Seth Godin, the popular marketing guru, has been saying? So where is the social evolution? Where is all the much touted, enlightened management that guys like Gary Hamel, the management expert, have been calling for?

The response appears to be that capitalism couldn't care less. It doesn't answer to the call for enlightenment. It works on a single-minded mode of operation. The calls to integrate an approach that encourages improvement derived from employee contribution aren't likely to be injected into a system where only one standard of success exists. What does human betterment have to do with maintaining profit when those pesky employees are just a necessary cost to the owners? Obviously, if you want to be a physician or an attorney there are prescribed educational paths. Other careers can be created through combinations of experience and course work. It is a falsehood to suggest that the applicability of one's education is the main, or only consideration in a huge array of types of work. The encouragements to package ourselves as creative, flexible, and always tech-savvy go far beyond any specific education credential. The subjective way these traits are framed still leave questions vague and unanswered.

How does one innovate and still stay tied to the rules of capitalism? You either work within the status quo, or you stand outside it and try your own experiments and hope that there isn't some law waiting to fall down on you and axe your plans. This is already happening with the birth of the sharing economy. For example, democratizing the rental landscape, whether rooms or rides, has been fraught with complaints from the already regulated industries who provide the same services. The existence of these new businesses seems like such a rightful step in evolution. If people are called on to be creative in making a life for themselves, the one they can no longer be assured of through ordinary means, then what would you expect but the formation of businesses like Uber, Lyft, and Airbnb?

It would seem disingenuous to claim that motivation is more critical for success in the absence of realities that make it fruitful. And yet popular pundits are utterly convinced, or at least want us to be, that people will be able to find new opportunities or create their own. How can we be led to think that we'll create our own jobs in a society that has already labeled the unemployed as losers? Even if it were possible to imagine a viable business, an entrepreneur still needs huge amounts resources and connections.

A Portfolio Career

If starting a business doesn't hold any appeal, you could sell your talents piecemeal through a number of different venues. This is called having a portfolio career. How modern is that? It appears to be feasible, but is it? The idea is to frame your talent and productive skill in a way that positions you to accept any of several different roles. This approach is called a portfolio because it is essentially a method of repackaging and freelancing clusters of related skills as opposed to the entire breadth of your curriculum vitae.

Though each of your activities requires a different range of skills, sometimes with no overlap between them, what you can create from them may still warrant a job offer. Outwardly it might seem unfocused and fragmented, but proponents of this idea claim the motivation for this mode of working is better work/life balance. The promoters of this idea seemed to think that employers would embrace the idea that candidates should be seen as a smorgasbord of talent. This notion ignores the importance placed on high specialization.

As a process for positioning or branding yourself, this approach might work if you're already adept at transferring your time and labor between different workplaces. In terms of efficacy, it raises the same questions as all the other forms of advice. Granted, there is no one definitive way to find work. I'm sure it is worthwhile to help people see alternative ways of presenting value to a potential employer or client. But this methodology seems to rehash and respin the same essential ingredients. The era of high unemployment has endured so long that the time has passed for attempting to develop more work search solutions.

The advice givers keep circulating their drivel. The unemployed are offered alternative ways of fitting into the economy. Meanwhile the system is already overloaded with their need, and simultaneously has no incentive to engage them. The excess of labor's capacity is an unfortunate consequence in a world that has mastered efficiencies, and where existing staff are already working fifty to seventy hours a week. The ways business must be conducted to ensure profit do not include requirements to retain labor beyond a point that is absolutely necessary. No wonder temporary contract workers are so appealing.

Aging out

Occasionally, counselors to the unemployed specify that their statements are geared more appropriately for those in the first quarter of their working lives. The field of expertise narrows considerably if the advice is for people in their mid-forties and older. There isn't a lot of conversation about what kind of work environments attract a person in the last third of their working lives. They are called on to possess traits such as attention to detail, fast paced work environment, and expresses sense of urgency. Rarely will a job seeker find requirements that ask for—deep thinker, always calm, able to hold together teams, create new systems and efficient procedure.

It is widely reported that nearly forty percent of the unemployed are forty-five and older. If they have not experienced disruption in their work lives before now they often don't realize the extent to which their age category targets them for premature dismissal. These random online observations are especially heartbreaking:

> I have not been in jail or prison, nor am I an
> alcoholic, drug addict or gambling addict. I am
> simply old, unemployed and out of money.

Until I aged out of the job market, I'd been hired for virtually every job for which I'd ever interviewed.

Power imbalance and beyond

It is the conduct of business that needs greater scrutiny.

There are those who can describe problems in the US economy perfectly, and put those problems into historical context that makes every event appear as an inevitable outcome. They also prescribe solutions for the masses of talented, highly trained people thrown to an economy that appears to operate on a survival of the fittest ethic. Very rarely does someone admit that the essential structure of capitalism simply doesn't require people to work if greater efficiencies of operation can eliminate the need for their labor. Conventional wisdom has mastered descriptive and prescriptive ways of talking about problems. All the while, this ignores critiquing the system at a deeper level. Sooner rather than later we'll need much better ways to figure out what to do with well-educated, working-age citizens that have nowhere to go and no viable businesses to start. Citizens will still need to be able to earn enough to afford new cars even when those vehicles can drive themselves. I don't see too many institutions or think tanks trying to figure out how we prepare for the other side of the double-edged technology sword. How will we account for what happens because of our lack of foresight?

Is it an assumption that employers retain their talent pool only to the extent that the company can squeeze as much out of them as possible? If so, this mindset also determines how labor is valued in other employment arrangements as well. In his book, *The New Deal at Work: managing the market driven workforce*, Peter Cappelli characterizes this as market-based employment transactions. This means short-term contracts, temporary staffing and outsourcing. Instead of mentoring and developing the career of employees in good standing, many employers have abandoned this investment in favor of placing career development responsibility on the individuals themselves. This creates an open field of people attempting to bridge the so-called skills gap on their own. This short-sighted approach on the employer's part sidelines people in mid-career and prejudices employers against the very people they've not retained. We are told that employers bemoan loss of values such as commitment and specialized skills. Yet, it is their readiness to abandon employees that creates the occasion of missing experience. Through the people I interviewed, I found plenty who could easily attest to this awkward situation. It leads to unemployed professionals having to make what amounts to educated guesses about the exact mix of skills and experience that employers want.

Conventional job hunting advice seems to maintain its credibility even in light of some pretty fundamental shifts in what is valued in the workplace. White collar work is valued as stable and respectable, and its very desirability makes the myth of mobility in the workplace hard to dispel. A typical work environment is rife with potential obstacles found in office politics and other interpersonal relationships. The barriers found in relational biases such as sexism, ageism, and probably any other ism you could think of, are intrinsically harder to battle. This complicates the exercise of authority within roles. It only takes a few players to perpetuate a workplace dysfunction, preventing others from raising issues about it.

It is harder to prove that meritocracy isn't working when its application has no standard bearer other than the opinion of a manager entrusted with the direction of human resources. These are resources mind you, not actual humans with their nasty subjective viewpoints.

Control, potential, untapped capacity

Some of the ways in which people relate to each other successfully or otherwise, create an atmosphere that upholds a certain tribal law within the team or organization. The unspoken rules of the pack make it much less likely that any one individual will have the courage to embrace what Nikil Saval calls the confrontational nature of organizing.

> When you do find successful organizing, it's often because the meritocratic basis of these workplaces seems to be totally eroded or severely undermined, as in the 1930s or with secretarial organizing in the 1970s.[1]

In his book, *Cubed: A Secret History of the Workplace*, Saval notes another factor that figures strongly in the success of organizing is the balance of supply and demand. To put it plainly, when labor markets are tighter it's easier for people to make demands. Industrial settings gave birth to labor unions because the abuses of power were so blatant. In white collar workplaces the abuses are equally blatant, but continue to live under the surface in attitudes and prejudices. It makes whistleblowers like Lilly Ledbetter all the more remarkable for the conviction she must have had in order to seek redress for years of being paid less than other equivalent staff members. (See the Lilly Ledbetter Fair Pay Act, January 29, 2009, the first piece of legislation signed by President Obama.)

It takes a powerful will to believe wholeheartedly in your own worth. Even now we seem to have such a poor understanding of what truly motivates people beyond a few simple dictates. We're handed a plate and told that the only thing on the menu is our salary range and our job title. From this meager meal we are supposed to arrive with all our integrity, passion, and creativity intact and ready to go. The enigma of our talent comes packaged as we define it, but if we allow our employment history to dictate how it is shaped, we will surely curtail much of its use. We may possess a well-grounded understanding of our talents within a given setting, but the ways in which to use them are restricted by the very nature of how businesses work. Richard Sennett talks about this in his book, *Respect in a World of Inequality.*

> New forms of work require people who are good at moving from task to task, job to job, place to place. In part this is due to shifting demand in the global marketplace; organizations must change their functions, business plans, and products on short notice. The ability to learn new things quickly becomes then of more value than the capacity to go ever deeper into an existing problem or body of data. And, since such an ability is worth more than fixed knowledge, the potential for learning is more serviceable than past achievement. This is the economic premium put on "potential ability."[2]

In this book Sennett gives the example of a piano competition judge struggling with assessing the contestants. They could display their mastery of technique, but often hesitated to take artistic risks and to that extent kept their potential restrained. (The respondents in my interviews have had experiences that suggest even if you demonstrate your nimbleness of intellect in acquiring and using new skills, if they come packaged in a fifty-something body they are about as well received as a regifted birthday present.)

The person with a known talent is asked to rely on the validity of judgments rendered from an authority figure. This assumes the person with the talent may not be reliable in assessing their own development, and that the assessment requires an external arbiter. It represents a great extension of faith to place this level of control in care of another person. Yet not everything that we call talent has a standard measurement against which it can be evaluated. So much of what succeeds in the context of human relationships is more accurately described as the flow of communication, of favorable feelings toward others, of confidence in the trust that people hold for each other. An atmosphere that lacks these crucial social elements tends to erode the well-being of those working in it. No level playing field exists in a workplace that hasn't yet established norms for upholding equitable treatment in the context of communication and trust. Nothing that I'm saying here is revolutionary. The statements are self-evident. But when you take a serious look at the precepts in which our society is rooted, it becomes clearer how its failures are inextricably bound up with our beliefs about human nature and its unwieldy components.

To ameliorate the human condition in relation to the vagaries of the labor market, one could start by questioning its requirements. Why does human labor require being in a market? Assessment of the quality of how well one labors is a marketplace in itself. The very act of placing labor in a market suggests that humans must accept the assessment in order to eat, have a place to live and everything else that supports life. For working people it is typically assumed that support needed outside the arena of wages, comes from family and charitable organizations. We've internalized and accepted this as the arrangement. This paradigm needs reversal. Shouldn't it be the other way around? You get to live. That is the given. What you choose to do beyond that is your labor and if a person aspires to a higher material plane, then one's work may increase to satisfy that aspiration. If others share your aspiration then so much the better for your outcome. None of this demands an assumption that greater amounts of material wealth for some necessarily means less for others. The only base assumption would be that everyone has a sufficiency to live without threat of deprivation. The necessity for pitting like-minded people against one another in competition for gaining a livelihood should be an artifact that remains in past centuries. It is not a problem-solving strategy, and predestines a rather dim view of humanity.

It says: We are so lazy that we'll hardly work even knowing that it is needful for our own benefit and the well-being of others. When we do work, our ultimate goal is primarily for greater material comfort in relation to all fellow humans in our sphere. The sphere now is not one extended family or individual village, but the entire globe. We have been working within the confinements of a competition mindset for so long that it has corrupted our ability to imagine a world without them. It is hardly surprising that the ways in which we frame success require a drive for dominance. As Sennett observes:

> For every Andrew Carnegie who emphasized rational management skills, there were many more Jay Goulds advocating sheer aggression and driving greed as the secret of business success. "Aptitude" meant simply a taste for competitive combat.[3]

The unavoidable common sense

So if I want to think clearly about real alternatives, what basic premise of the labor market will still accommodate me? The labor market is part of a larger relationship between companies and individuals as they are regulated by government. Its stability has eroded as the ruling class progressively removed the ability of government to restrict corporate greed. In turn, workers are over burdened with needing to know how to maintain a healthy relationship with the labor market. This is especially true in the contingent workforce. Technology has brought us to a point where we are able to produce goods and services with much less human power. Full employment may not be an achievable end in this scenario. The only model still circulating is to tell people to work for wages even when reality doesn't support this probability. The means with which to live need to sit on stable ground. The labor market and its remediation through government, i.e. unemployment insurance, is clearly not enough. And it won't be as more and more automation and robotics command space once used by human labor.

Having achieved that fantasied, abundant society leaves us to create a system that fairly distributes the resources of a basic, decent life—food, shelter, and healthcare. After all, it is not the fault of otherwise laboring people if their jobs have been outsourced or disappeared. The chase for cheaper labor across the planet has reached the ends of the earth.

So much unused labor allows the imbalance of power to fall in favor of employers. Because of this there still exists a need for forms of collective bargaining. Would there be a need for collective bargaining if rules of engagement in work were defended as vigorously for individuals as corporate interests? An astute observer will understand that corporations are licensed by the state and should be required to show a benefit to society in return for the privileges they are granted. The idea that creating money is the only required benefit constricts other possible forms of value. The requirement of incorporation could be to prove your organization's intended purpose for solving real world problems. This might set up a paradigm shift that would accelerate a ripple effect of improvements. Rather than manufacturing pretense and convincing people they can't live without it, organizations would start looking, and hopefully behaving, very differently. If corporations were discouraged from rewarding only shareholders and executives, the balance of power could be redressed. Part of the correction would come from making adjustments in work currently paid with insufficient wages, and inadequate taxation of corporate profits. Corporations support the community through taxes on their profits. This can't happen if those taxes are not collected or are evaded through the use of loopholes. The rate of taxation that applies to earned income must have a corollary assessment on corporate income. If capitalism cannot be abandoned, how should it survive without restrictions and revisions like these? Capitalism may not be in process of collapse, but the society based on how it is currently practiced is in need of an overhaul in order to redress so many inequities.

The economic system is supposed to be based on a flow of demand for goods and services. The way capitalism is implemented now mandates a concentration of wealth in the hands of the owners. In order to achieve that, efficiency means reducing or eliminating labor costs, and this effectively strangles that flow. You've got masses of people struggling to partake in the rewards of their own productivity that has essentially been stolen from them. As professor William Domhoff of UC Santa Cruz puts it:

> You can't have a vital economic system when it's designed to be the circular flow of capital, labor, supply and demand yet the entities who are supposed to provide jobs strive to eliminate them while also siphoning as much of the wealth as possible out of the system.[4]

Traditional business versus new business: Can it be done?

What is the flip side to the problem with pundits who are always trying to create a new formulary for their pharmacy of advice? Rather than looking at what the employees should do, what does the business itself purport to do? What is its stated purpose, and does it believe that the process by which it brings it products to market is just as important as why?

I didn't arrive at this question on my own. I discovered Rosabeth Moss Kanter, a professor of business at Harvard. November 2011, in an article for the *Harvard Business Review* she made some pretty bold and refreshing observations. She talked about how companies who want to build enduring institutions are better served if they operate from what she calls a social or institutional logic. The standard version of capitalism forces companies to ignore the power of their command of resources to influence the lives of employees and customers alike. It is a lopsided belief that says the sole purpose of business is to make money.

Companies who are high-performing and admired she says, find ways to develop practices where "people are not afterthoughts or inputs to be used and discarded."[5] I considered this critique, and could hardly believe that someone from an institution like Harvard would submit an argument that for some old-school guys must sound like treason. Yet, the exercise of capitalism enforces a one-sided view of production. Companies do not have to account for how they despoil labor any more than they have to account for pollution created from producing their goods. Reading this article was an opportunity to hear someone at last speak a vital truth. A truly enlightened company understands its role as a vehicle for providing decent livelihoods, and sustaining the conditions that allow them to flourish beyond the measures of short-term profits.

Seventy-three comments followed this online article. They were a perfect example of the conflicting opinions people maintain even when they appear to be giving these ideas the benefit of the doubt. Sadly, some of the comments also showed a deeply entrenched viewpoint. One commenter even claimed that making money itself was enlightened self-interest, and reason enough to be considered a good thing. Another one suggested that he wake up and see that value is measured by more than money. And so it goes.

Again, I've raised more questions than I've answered. I've looked as far as I can go from a computer screen. I've dropped hints, made suggestions, and sneered at human foibles when overwhelmed by the absurdities. In the process of performing this mental exercise I've had the opportunity to expose some nagging thoughts. I've tested them out to see if they were reason enough to think that my fate hinged on their existence. I have since reasoned that the answer is—no. I am guilty, though, of giving some of them too much power over my state of mind.

One can stand and stir the pot for only so long. Sooner or later the fire dies, the pot grows cold, and you have to pull off the witch's hat and look elsewhere for better incantations. The next chapter represents an oasis of contemplation far from the polarized dialogue of the fate of capitalism. It is in some of these proposals that I find the greatest source of understanding if not solace for my long-wandering heart.

Chapter five
Rescuers and reasoners

This chapter is about the process of revising the mindset that hasn't served the person using it. This is about moving thoughts away from all the forms of how to do this or that, and redirecting attention. The writers I focus on now compassionately explained how to extricate myself from the conditions by which I had felt so constricted. They reconfigured quandaries and helped me regain strength and conviction that I had a life not only worth living, but a necessary one.

What is a mindset? It is the collection of beliefs and attitudes on which you base your actions. It also predicts a lot about how you will react when those beliefs are not verified by your own experience. If they remain unconfirmed your beliefs will take the natural course of eroding and lose any power they may have had to influence your future actions. Without these convictions you either have to deal with the emptiness in the wake of their dissolution or actively seek replacements for them. If you choose to seek replacements for something you previously accepted as a given, it helps to have a sense of where to look. I went about this with the shotgun approach. I let my intellectual curiosity and natural inclinations guide me in discovering the authors I studied. Most of the writers I found were psychologists, teachers, and philosophers. Some were even economic behaviorists. Their works, as I pieced them together, revealed more accurately the world as I saw it.

It was this process of replacing the old beliefs with some new ideas that built a stronger foundation for my mental health. These authors dissected and clarified bits and pieces of truth about the apparatus regarding merit and work. From the tangle of what I had experienced firsthand, they rescued me from guilt, rage, and shame. My mind mellowed for having found others who critiqued the world in a way that appeared well-reasoned, intelligent, thorough, and most of all accurate.

Churning through all the job search commentators left me stuck in my state of mind as well as my circumstances. I was supposed to be getting over it; so why didn't I feel like that was ever going to happen? Miraculously, for everything I questioned someone had already studied the phenomenon and proposed an explanation. I found sociologists and psychologists who could put my anecdotal experiences into a larger context. This was the world I could not see, the one hiding in tiny thoughts, and circulating behind theories of success. In every strata of life existed some form of disruption that I had already experienced.

At the internal, molecular level, Daniel Goleman, the psychologist who wrote *Emotional Intelligence*, informed me about the inner workings of my brain. I felt like a changed person, and indeed I was, thanks to something known as the HPA axis. The acronym is derived from the first letter of each of three glands, the hypothalamus, pituitary, and adrenal. This powerful triumvirate expresses hormones that influence reactions to stimuli. The infamous processor of emotions, the amygdala, controls our survival instinct. When triggered, it engages the HPA axis. The rush of hormones from these glands changes how the brain prioritizes information. In times of fear this means that everything relevant to what is scaring us locks our attention. It activates a hierarchy of memory formation so that we remember and think about only the agent causing our fear in the moment. The brain doesn't require actual physical threats to feel this level of fear. The symbolic reality that confronts us every day is enough to keep us in the grip of distressing emotions. As a person's attention narrows and fixates on their fear, they become unable to function optimally, let alone experience genuine well-being.

I was definitely in the grip of derailment at the biological level. Layered on top of this road block was knowing that regardless of my feelings about it, I was still conscripted to go into the world and recreate a role for myself. But as I was to discover only in retrospect, I was losing my desire even to continue going through the job search turnstile. Find a position in a good company, no matter how precarious, and stay there as long as you can because you are not allowed to depend on it, and you may be doing this again someday. It is a glib attitude that tells us not to depend on a sense of job security. You must function optimally regardless of any level of fear you may be experiencing. The independent agent is supposed to agree to attitudes that reinforce the view of her work engagement as vulnerable. This just makes the repercussions of job loss worse. Your work can't really be considered a livelihood if you are intended always to think of it as short-term. The inherent conflict runs much deeper than simply advising someone not to be so reliant on certainty. Most features of life are uncertain and yet everyday fluctuations that mar our well-being don't produce the same level of crisis as job loss. It is as if we are being told that the importance of our problems are all the same when we know they are not. The very nature of contingent work belies the importance of it to both employer and employee. The schism makes us aware of living outside of the typical permanent salaried position. The time management required by being in a subcategory of worker risks making us resentful. So add a dollop of anger to that fear and you've got a poor place to start rebuilding a life.

The myth of meritocracy

So let's say you have succeeded in avoiding the rut of rumination into which your brain might have fallen. What other trains of thought will zoom right past you without your comprehension of their cargo? Here is where Alain de Botton and Richard Sennett unpack a few ideas.

My premise is that we all endure the human condition without understanding what we have agreed to, and that is most apparent in our need to embrace absolutes. Many people will insist that they got to where they are because of their own hard work. One could be talked out of a limb sooner than relinquish the thought that anything but hard work was the reason for material success. But if you examine this notion, as de Botton has, you may see the weakness of its inference.

We are practically mandated to believe that we're in control of our destinies. Our self-esteem is bolstered when that belief in control is reinforced by success. It feeds our optimism and in turn reinforces our belief that progress is based on ability and talent rather than on class privilege or wealth. People adhere to the idea of meritocracy even in the face of dubious evidence. As de Botton puts it:

> It is completely crazy to imagine that we will ever reach a society where people will really deserve their success and totally deserve their failure. There are simply too many factors in anyone's life, and to expect that you can simply take a reading of anyone's life and determine from that whether they deserve to be there or not is simply unbelievable.[6]

For a charming comparison of belief systems de Botton tells us that the ancient Romans believed good outcomes were the gifts of the goddess of Fortune. The gift says nothing of the person upon which it was bestowed. The person doesn't own it and should simply be grateful for the gift.

If the prevalence of our control is the source of success then it also demands that we see failure as a personal point of blame. It is so much easier to agree to the absolute nature of yes and no than to suffer reality. We are more comfortable weighing a contrast of opposites. To frame life as effort versus laziness helps you avoid the vagaries of a thousand unknowns over which there is no control. To make peace with everything you can't control would be to exhibit a level of tolerance even Buddha would admire.

For another perspective on the dark side of meritocracy I turn to Mr. Sennett. As I mentioned in the previous chapter, the assumption in the corporate world is that associates will take responsibility for their own career development. Once a certain level of expertise has been attained, and the expert is released to the labor market, there is yet another obstacle in front of the candidate. In a discussion of what he calls the decline of the skills society, Sennett asserts that there is a huge emphasis on talent search in the name of meritocracy. As the staffing agency searches for a candidate, there is a presumption that talent is scarce. The ability to do good work is only in the hands of the unusually gifted. This cultural ethos sets up an environment of neglect.

In order to understand what is meant by neglect, you have only to imagine what we already know of responses to job openings. The agent is faced with several dozen candidates, any one of whom could produce excellent work. As a result, the talent search is exalted for producing an exemplar of some rare set of skills found only in a single person. Meanwhile the other two dozen equally wonderful individuals remain in limbo, their skills declining, and thus neglected. The majority of available jobs do not require being unusually gifted, and yet the search is for the purple squirrel. According to the urban dictionary, purple squirrel is a metaphor used by recruiters to identify the unrealistic expectations of a client company—where only the exceptional candidate who exactly matches the qualifications and experience will be considered for a job opening.

This ongoing scenario perpetuates a view of the non-corporately engaged person as some degraded version of human capital. It is as if the understanding of skill development has been abandoned. The old-world version requires time, persistence, and a term Sennett uses, embodiment, the nature of deep habitual thinking. This version of skill development is the result of the infamous 10,000 hour rule. But with all the emphasis on innovation as the direct route to creating value, where is there time to apply this rule? Does someone have to spend that many hours in addition to, or outside of the hours required to make a living?

From negative effects at the molecular level and restrictive hiring practices at the social level, my internet wanderings also led me to psychologists such as Adam Philips and Bruce Levine. I listened to them discuss common frustrations on an individual and collective level, and found validation of my own reactions.

I thought the nature of aspiration was a simple, linear progression, as if all one could want was styled after a pyramid as easily partitioned as the four food groups or an organizational chart. My aspirations were now so mangled I didn't want to be associated with them for the guilt they caused me. So it was easy to agree with Phillips who suggests that we need "better pictures of satisfaction." Rather than chasing after ever illusive ideals, we'd be better off having more realistic ideas of what makes a good life, one that is genuinely attainable. Ideals, he tells us, are set up to make one fail. They create fight or flight responses in us. You may chase after some ideal version of how life should be, or you may find yourself running away from it, getting rid of it, producing another one, or complying and doing battle with it. I had never heard anyone describe the frustration of desire as something we value. But I understood this was what I was doing. When I read *Missing Out: In Praise of the Unlived Life*, I recognized that feature in myself.

It wasn't as if I wanted more rules to live by, or to believe in yet another authority on such and such. I was satisfied simply by notions that made sense to me. Like a child who takes pride in no longer believing in Santa Claus, I could claim comprehension of strange twists in the human psyche still unknown to others. I was becoming the professor of my own life, observing my reactions to the turmoil, and finally making peace with the sense of being on the outside looking in.

I entertained the idea, as Phillips suggests, that we lead two parallel lives: the life we actually live and the one that we wish for. My acquaintance with what I wished for seemed like a junkyard I was forced to revisit every time I wrote a cover letter. I began to see it as comedy, but I also realized the one I actually lived was neglected. I wanted to stop seeing myself as desperate or struggling.

It was around this time that I discovered Bruce Levine. In his book, *Get up, Stand up: uniting populists, energizing the defeated and battling the corporate elite*, I heard the voice of someone who could characterize exactly how people struggle to keep their lives intact. Here was a psychologist who didn't hesitate to defend the normal reactions of people in times of crisis.

> There is nothing more important in breaking people from their capacity to resist oppressive forces than creating a society of isolated people. With social isolation, people stop sharing information, there is an absence of mutual validation about the source of their misery, and they are much more likely to believe that it is their personal weakness that has allowed them to be victimized.[7]

I resisted admitting that this was my pattern of behavior as well. But my gratitude for his wisdom continued to well up page after page. Levine accurately describes so many aspects of our culture that lead to weakened social connections. He expertly correlates specific emotional environments to negative effects as they are experienced collectively.

> ...believing that you are totally dependent on others undermines your sense of self, as though you are a child in an adult's body. People who feel completely dependent on others are likely to turn over decision-making power to those others, the precise mind-set that corporate and government elites most love to see.[8]

From my point of view these observations seemed undeniable. Without evaluating the milieu in which we have to survive we then only have ourselves to blame for failures. What Levine was saying seemed to validate my thinking. It was pointless to make judgments independent of really understanding the mechanisms supporting the corporate state. If you are forced to accept that the work you depend on requires treating you as disposable, then your stability will have to be drawn from somewhere else. This sets us up for what Levine calls the destruction of collective self-confidence. The obliteration of self-reliance feeds our sense of inadequacy. When the things beyond our control are so immense, our focus narrows smaller and smaller as we feel less effective. After *Get up, Stand up*, I felt I had finally read something true to my experience with the forces governing capitalism and corporatism, for I have no better way of describing it. His book proved to be a complementary work to many other psychologists and philosophers I had been studying for years.

Hidden treasure from the spiritual Zen chakra poet diva gods and goddesses... Alan Watts, David Whyte, Caroline Myss, Charles Eisenstein, and Mihalyi Csikszentmihalyi and others

These writers suggested ways to use a better version of intelligence. They had a way of imagining the world through the expression of psychic energy blanketing the collective consciousness holding the invisible network together. They made observations that link individual behaviors to collective ones, and illuminate how we frustrate our desires by inadequately and dishonestly framing what really keeps us stymied. For example, there are so many restricted ways in which we conceive of our lives in terms of vocation, ambition and aptitude. The social pressures that influence our process of making choices do not necessarily come from a place that holds our best interest above all else. The general approach we are encouraged to have is one of a conquering, competitive nature. We're encouraged to believe no other impetus will be sufficient to launch us into this world. And so it becomes a comical play of opposites if, in fact, our genuine desire is to remain in a noncombative role with the world of others. How do you go about accepting your true nature? Our friend, Alan Watts, invites us to set forth in life with two fundamental presuppositions: 1) you are not going to improve the world, and 2) you are not going to improve yourself. If you flow parallel with these two ideas then you already have a better perspective. The result may be that when you give up the idea of being in combat with the forces of competition, you will have freed up the energy you need to face challenges of your own choosing rather than ones defined for you. Nonetheless, it is impossible to avoid the pitfalls of our subjective way of perceiving the world. We feel first and think second. What I now understood about the appearance of intrinsic conflict in the workplace, forced me to disregard most, if not all, identity with it. If I was in a competition and everything I knew about self-promotion still wasn't working, then I'd have to change my whole approach. My transformation required so much more than a new mental space. As the Irish poet, David Whyte, has characterized:

> Becoming visible to the world through our
> work seems to be a central necessity in a voca-
> tion. The more invisible we feel, the more un-
> heard, unseen, unheeded, the more dissatisfied

we seem to be and the more **unreal** we seem
to ourselves.[9]

To unreal I would add misled, and the sense that one's
wholeness is fated for inevitable disintegration. Not only did
this seem true in a vocational sense, but it proved a huge challenge to disconnect material well-being from this equation. If
you take having to work for granted, then your self-evaluation
in light of the realities of wage slavery will leave you panic
stricken. The unavoidable existential questions just pile on:
Was I really developing a better sense of what I control and
what I do not? How do you develop that better sense? What
are the realities behind the beliefs you take for granted? Are
you burdened by holding out for something that is actually a
falsehood?

The rescue from at least some of this pedantic inquiry
could only have come from writers who took a view far from
the predominance of the material world. My attention gravi-
tated toward those who could speak wisely about the interconnectedness of all humanity. It is difficult to explain the sense
of relief I felt as I have listened repeatedly to the work of
Caroline Myss. Maybe this is what truth feels like:

> We are kidding ourselves to think a positive at-
> titude is sufficient to navigate these waters. It is
> not. The current system cannot hold us intact.
> We are not facing problems. Problems have
> solutions. We are facing predicaments. Predic-
> aments don't have solutions. They sweep us up
> with them, and they reshape us. We have for
> centuries worshipped at the altar of reason. We
> thought reason was the key to everything, that
> we could reason with God. We've reached the
> end of the age of reason.[10]

It is from this writer that I found confirmation of the very
path I had traveled and what it meant in the deepest sense:

> Your spirit must experience the inadequacy of
> the power of the outside world to serve you
> in any way in an effective manner. Your spirit
> must awaken to the power of your psyche over
> the power of the physical world.[11]

Her words assured me that if I was looking for a deeper sense of order, its only source would come from the power that lies within. I knew this as a common teaching, and have come to understand it from the space left clear and open after the dissolution of the life I thought would never change. The life where I would always bounce back, always have a way to be self-sufficient, no longer existed. The empty space made me feel infantilized and too self-conscious. Slowly the nakedness of that self, though still raw, was losing its sensitivity to the new reality before me. I had to accept that whatever life I could create for myself in the future wouldn't be achieved using the old presuppositions. I didn't really believe I was getting tougher, but I was losing my ability to care about the parts of me that were already sloughing off. I could see now taking one more look at my old self was just an excuse to poke the embers, checking for residual heat in a rage that was ending its life cycle.

So where does all this newly acquired perspective leave you? The need to move on persists. I'm a woman in my fifties who hasn't been attached to the corporate world for many years. It wasn't easy to dismiss my identification with work. If I wanted to be engaged in a different way of living and being I had to embrace another spirit. I had to internalize a public persona befitting an intelligent, creative person still in touch with her gifts and talents. And all this stood before me following a period in my life where I was cut off from professional working relationships where I might have experienced feedback and confirmation of my contribution or acknowledgment to reinforce my sense of worth. I had to rebuild it on my own. When you've operated from a wounded place for so long, it takes a major internal shift to reorient yourself. You have to see yourself in a social environment where reciprocity is the real currency. How you imagine your strength in trading that new currency is your ability to believe your connection and power to contribute is just as strong as anyone's. I'd have to envision a way to maintain a sense of empowerment that could not be breached. In order to free myself from self-critical ruminations, I had to allow that not only were there no authorities on adulthood who knew better than I did, I also had to stop imagining that they'd appear, that they existed at all. I had to become comfortable with being the sole creator and inheritor of everything I thought, said, or did—a terrifying, but exhilarating possibility. It seems laughably obvious, but look beyond the obvious. A rupture with the previous incarnation of your persona will leave nothing but doubts in a mind obliterated from identification or connection with the world. Building a new way mentally to live in the world is not a task anyone would embrace if they didn't have to for reasons of sanity.

I had already experienced the inadequacy of the power of the outside world to serve me, as Myss so eloquently puts it. Now I took that idea one step further, and absorbed the work of Mihalyi Csikzentmihalyi from *The Evolving Self: A psychology for the third millennium.*

In search of a life worth living

In this book Csikzentmihalyi looks at societal development from an historical point of view, and maps out the norms around which cultures develop. Individuals, always having to take their cues from the environment culture supplies, have to identify with those norms. He deftly explains the difficulty inherent in this identification and how much culture curtails a wider view of human possibility by constantly making delineations between us and them.

We take such false pride in thinking that we are independent of the conditions and events that bring others down, always thinking that we are separate, different, or better. These thoughts are a poor shield that only keep us from ourselves. We are not regularly offered authentic ways to achieve autonomy and remain in a healthy frame of mind. And yet it requires a nimble, malleable mind to accept a future that always appears murky and indefinable where goals are concerned.

The whole of society, if it is evolving, is actively engaged in shaping the predominant thoughts and behavior away from the past and into the future. But this is why it is so difficult:

> The past–represented by the determinism of the instincts, the weight of tradition, the desires of the self–is always stronger. The future– represented by the ideals of a life that is freer, more compassionate, more in tune with the reality that transcends our needs–is by necessity weaker, for it is an abstraction, a vision of what might be.[12]

In order to improve upon their current state of being the components of systems have to find a balancing harmony between differentiation and integration.

> Differentiation refers to the degree to which a system is composed of parts that differ in structure or function from one another. Integration refers to the extent to which the different parts communicate and enhance one another's goals.[13]

When you have a high degree of differentiation and integration, the system is described as complex. Complexity is a central theme in evolution because systems that are more sophisticated have the advantage in solving problems. It is no easy task to use these principles consistently to manifest a society functioning at a peak level. In chapter six, "Directing Evolution," Csikzentmihalyi illustrates how Russia and the US have dis-integrated in opposite ways—one for stifling personal initiative, the other for erosion of common values.

No wonder that anyone in search of a better control of their consciousness has so few role models to draw from. The distillation of these principles expressed at an individual level means that a person must choose how to expend different forms of psychic energy. In my case, I had given too much significance to the power of flawed systems over my health and livelihood. One needs to avoid becoming self-absorbed, and simultaneously not too concerned about conformity to norms of conduct, especially if those norms are reflective of a larger, deleterious trend in the culture.

> But it is almost impossible to live a decent life when the social system is devoted to greed and blind exploitation. And to change the system, one needs to step out of the cocoon of personal goals and confront larger issues in the public arena.[14]

I was constantly struck by the level of detail Csikzentmihalyi could elucidate on this topic. In many of his books, he champions themes of individuals becoming independent of their social environments while maintaining an ability to love life regardless of external circumstances. This was the process that consumed me. I had to make peace with so many weaknesses.

It was a painful process to become independent of these environments. I grew up in a robust, but splintered Catholic family where the stress of figuring out all the rules left no energy to figure out if there needed to be a place for me in them. Avoidance was the key to staying unharmed. While that way of thinking worked in childhood, it was positively ruinous in adulthood, where one is rewarded for the capacity to take a stand and defend it. The impulse to remain unknown and out of critical fire will deter a young person's development when they are thrust upon the adult stage. The effort it takes to reverse that impulse will consume a lifetime.

But so often we are schooled to believe that rewards in life come only from the external circumstances of those social environments. As we imbue our minds with this shallow truth, we rob ourselves of the deeper, truer ones that might save us from wasting our time with despair over the loss of those circumstances.

Isn't the popularity of yoga and meditation a very telling phenomenon? We are encouraging each other to chill out and find our own way of living life with style and grace. Running parallel with this are the same old enticements to work hard, win someone over, get new customers, produce something faster, better, stronger, bigger. The external is always the most predictable form. No wonder so many are still held in thrall to it. Someone of my generation, by the very nature of this phase of life, becomes interested in deeper, richer experiences, and the craving for validation from others holds less power over us. At this point, we are looking to confirm what we have already chosen to believe about the human condition. If we are lucky, that still includes love and relationships that help us face the future, and a desire to be a participant in making a better life true for others as well.

There is yet another author who explains how to make a new story true for ourselves and others. The work of Charles Eisenstein is mesmerizing in its ability to characterize the cause and effect of individual turmoil and its collective expression. In his work, *The More Beautiful World Our Hearts Know is Possible*, he illustrates what happens when we no longer have the will to participate in a society constantly pushing us to work harder at fitting into the conventional paradigm.

> ...the old story isn't motivating you anymore.
> What once made sense, no longer makes sense.
> You are beginning to withdraw from that world. Society does its best to persuade you to resist that withdrawal, which, when resisted, is called depression. [15]

I wasn't persuaded. After remaining hopeful about the possibilities, my distance from stable, full-time work was long enough that I couldn't imagine how it would ever be recreated. That was the old story. Half-hearted attempts at recreating a career weren't going to work. They couldn't. I would have to find a new story, and a compelling sense of purpose. In the old system you can't have gaps in your resume, you must have accomplishments, and references who can speak about you from recent history. In a new conception of a personal history, your best work would have to speak for itself over time. I often feared that I'd never get past the requirements of those living in the old story. That was where the majority of people still seemed to live. Now my work would have to include a renewed level of courage in order to pull myself from the Age of Separation, as Eisenstein puts it.

Throughout the industrial age the typical world view was ordered and structured according to the perceptions and will of human dominance over nature. It is the consequences of this world view that Eisenstein dissects through a series of thirty-six essays. These arguments echo many of the themes brought up in the works of Myss, Levine, and Csikzentmihalyi. We take for granted seeing ourselves as separate from others who struggle equally in a hostile universe populated by impersonal forces and competing individuals. To relieve ourselves from alienation we must then believe in a sacred source outside of ourselves—which is yet another separation we recognize. In order to create a new world we'll have to figure out how to embrace the interconnectedness of all things in a way we've never succeeded in doing before. A beautiful, possible world is described in these essays. There are many ways in which we can recognize that we have created these illusions of separation, and only we can heal the self-inflicted wounds from this story. We are the ones who must take responsibility for the false divisions keeping us from living harmoniously in the world.

At this point, it feels as if I have circumnavigated the globe to come back to a place all these authors have inextricably led me. Each one served their purpose. Each one provided a necessary step back to wholeness. Any day I recognize some mysterious synchronicity that leads me to solve a problem or meet the right person who just happens to share something I needed to know is one more day when fear doesn't win. This is the essence of an individual evolution. The work that follows requires maintaining a consciousness fully open and fully alert. I will not soon forget the many cautionary notes of these writers, as Csikzentmihalyi reminds us:

> ...it is mandatory that we understand how much of our psychic energy is channeled away by those who drain our lives to enrich theirs.[16]

I am devoted to the task of channeling energy. Throughout this process I've often wanted to distill my learnings to a few well-chosen words that I could always come back to as the benchmark of honest reasoning. I found it one day at the end of a lecture Sam Harris once gave about free will. It goes like this:

> We are linked to each other, and our past, and to history.
> We are part of a system, and therefore what we do matters.
> You can't take credit for your talents, but it matters that you use them.
> You can't really be blamed for your weaknesses, but it matters that you correct them.
> So pride and shame don't make a lot of sense in the final analysis.
> But they weren't much fun anyway. These are isolating emotions.
> What does make sense is a commitment to well-being and improving your life

and the lives of others.
Love and compassion make sense.[17]

Amen.

Epilogue
The possibility of improved choices

If there is a next phase, it would be in visions of the future. A work of nonfiction is supposed to solve a problem. The author's attempt to do this is what drives the narrative. I still don't have the solution to these problems, but I have at least discovered a few people who have thought about the closest alternatives.

Just as I found people who work toward understanding social evolution, there are as many who have plans and workable ideas for creating a world with greater participatory ease. Suggested ways to direct change work together to structure a system that values and supports all participants. These economists talk about ways that would keep the world well maintained and at a human scale, constantly flowing, and self-corrective through means that are built-in to the process.

Since starting this project I've been listening to Richard Wolff talk about worker self-directed enterprises. David Harvey talks about a money system that doesn't reward accumulation. Gar Alperovitz champions worker cooperatives. My favorite is Guy Standing, a professor at the University of London. He understands the life that people live when faced with repeatedly having to look for work. He calls this group the precariat.

> The people in the precariat have no corporate narrative to give to their lives. And more importantly than that, they have no occupational narrative to give to their lives. I am becoming something. I am something. They can't do that. You might find them doing something now and three months later you ask the same person and they're doing something completely different. [18]

As he describes the effects of these conditions he also interjects some very interesting historical perspective.

> This is the first class in history that has a level of education that is higher than the expected level of labor they have to perform—what we used to call invisible under employment.[19]

> The people in the precariat suffer from not what the old proletariat experienced in the 60s and 70s, but uncertainty, unknown unknowns.[20]

Until I started listening to Guy Standing, I wasn't sure there was anyone who really, thoroughly understood what people in this group were experiencing. Only someone who knows this much detail could have the courage to suggest guaranteed basic income as a solution. A discussion on that topic is completely worthwhile, but well beyond the scope of this book. However, the fact that it is even gaining traction as a topic of discussion says a lot about what might be possible.

Another possibility exists within the very way finance is conceived and promoted. There is an organization called The Capital Institute that wants to do this. They reimagine what a better functioning version of capitalism may look like via the eight principles of what they call "regenerative capitalism." Some of the revisions this organization supports relate to empowered participation so that you have the authority to negotiate for your own needs. They also concede that the circulation of money, information and the efficient use and reuse of materials is particularly critical. The Capital Institute created a project they call the field guide to investing in a regenerative economy. I pulled a quote from their video that strikes me as a vital part of the conversation: "People are just not going to be able to adopt a new consciousness, a new paradigm, if they can't act on it."

So true. We need something we can act upon, and I am no exception. This conversation seems endless, and having come to the conclusion of my story, there are any number of ways to end it. I can't claim victory over any of the experiences I've mentioned here. Even as these issues remain unresolved, I feel encouraged to know there are people like Guy Standing and John Fullerton (from Capital Institute) who are at least suggesting what should be done. I'm not sure how to go about being part of the solution to the world's problems. I'm not even sure how to solve the ones remaining in the life I have left to live. There are days when I am convinced that taking a solving-a-problem point of view is the wrong stance entirely. Maybe the time has come to look on the other side of the door and stop calling it a problem. It's time to get busy doing something else. Reflection works as long as the image you see coming back at you becomes larger than the one staring into it. My image of the world now includes people I've never met, but at least I've found some with thoughts, ideas, and solutions that are grounded, sane, and compassionate. It's a start.

Notes

1   Jake Blumgart, "White Collar Blues: An Interview With Nikil Saval," *Jacobin Magazine,* May 20, 2014, https://www.jacobinmag.com/2014/05/white-collar-blues-an-interview-with-nikil-saval/

2   Richard Sennett, *Respect in a World of Inequality*, W. W. Norton & Company, Inc., New York, 2003, p. 80.

3   Ibid. p. 79.

4   G. William Domhoff, "Who Rules America? Power in America - Wealth, Income, and Power" University of California at Santa Cruz, http://www2.ucsc.edu/whorulesamerica/power/wealth.html

5   Rosabeth Moss Kanter, "How Great Companies Think Differently," *Harvard Business Review*, November 2011, http://hbr.org/2011/11/how-great-companies-think-differently/ar/1

6   Alain de Boton, "On Pessimism," YouTube accessed 01/03/14, https://www.youtube.com/watch?v=Aw1oLtuJO-XQ

7   Bruce Levine, *Get up, Stand up: uniting populists, energizing the defeated and battling the corporate elite*, Chelsea Green Publishing, White River Junction, VT, 2011, p. 68.

8   Ibid. p. 71.

9   David Whyte, *The Three Marriages: Reimagining Work, Self and Relationship*, Riverhead Books, New York, 2009, p. 288.

10   Caroline Myss, "Freedom of Humbleness, Finding your Light, Mystical path and grace," YouTube accessed 01/08/14, https://www.youtube.com/watch?v=GARZ-KhEMNOo

11   Caroline Myss, "Chakras part 11, Carolyn answers questions from the audience," YouTube accessed 01/08/14, https://www.youtube.com/watch?v=GF2yyH3jLpQ

12   Mihalyi Csikszentmihalyi, *The Evolving Self: A psychology for the third millennium*, HarperCollins Publishers, Inc., New York, 1993, p. 161.

13   Ibid. p. 156.

14   Ibid. p. 281.

15   Charles Eisenstein, *The More Beautiful World Our Hearts Know is Possible*, North Atlantic Books, Berkeley, CA, 2013, p. 124.

16   Csikszentmihalyi, *The Evolving Self*, 114.

17   Sam Harris, "On Free Will," YouTube accessed 01/04/14, https://www.youtube.com/watch?v=pCofmZl-C72g

18   Guy Standing, "A Precariat Charter: From denizens to citizens, a seminar with Guy Standing," YouTube accessed 6/20/2015 https://www.youtube.com/watch?v=RGLSGeqF-1Po

19   Ibid.

20   Ibid.